ALL THE WORLD IS A STAGE

Unlock Your Inner Gifts

SUSAN B. SMALL

© Copyright Susan B. Small 2022 - All rights reserved.

The content contained within this book may not be reproduced, duplicated or transmitted without direct written permission from the author or the publisher.

Under no circumstances will any blame or legal responsibility be held against the publisher, or author, for any damages, reparation, or monetary loss due to the information contained within this book. Either directly or indirectly. You are responsible for your own choices, actions, and results.

Legal Notice:

This book is copyright protected. This book is only for personal use. You cannot amend, distribute, sell, use, quote or paraphrase any part, or the content within this book, without the consent of the author or publisher.

Disclaimer Notice:

Please note the information contained within this document is for educational and entertainment purposes only. All effort has been executed to present accurate, up to date, and reliable, complete information. No warranties of any kind are declared or implied. Readers acknowledge that the author is not engaging in the rendering of legal, financial, medical or professional advice. The content within this book has been derived from various sources. Please consult a licensed professional before attempting any techniques outlined in this book.

By reading this document, the reader agrees that under no circumstances is the author responsible for any losses, direct or indirect, which are incurred as a result of the use of the information contained within this document, including, but not limited to, — errors, omissions, or inaccuracies.

For Harrison and Oliver

About the Author

SUSAN B SMALL is a wife, proud mother of 2 sons, and a Nain (Welsh for grandmother). She has had the privilege of being an educator for fifty years, and the honor of serving as a team member on several volunteer organizations, supporting deserving children in Africa, India, Nepal, and the Philippines. In her adolescence, she began to question the 'unfairness' of life, especially for children, animals, and nature. Susan considers herself to be a 'seeker' on a spiritual journey. ALL THE WORLD IS A STAGE is a collection of her learnings and reflections on what LIFE has taught her and to which she is eternally grateful.

Contents

Your Journey

Your job is not who you are,
Your car is not who you are,
Your looks are not who you are,
Not even your body is who you are,
You are simply on a journey,
Just trying things out,
To see what you like,
To see what you do not like,
Because you can,
Because its temporary,
And because
It is all on the way
HOME.

MIKE DOOLEY

All The World Is A Stage

ALL THE WORLD IS A STAGE is a compilation of ideas, thoughts, reflections, quotes, and a script for the reader to contemplate with an open mind.

> *All the world's a stage,*
> *And all the men and women merely*
> *players;*
> *They have their exits and their entrances;*
> *And one man in his time plays many parts*

WILLIAM SHAKESPEARE

YOUR LIFE JOURNEY IS YOUR ROLE IN THE universal script.

YOU are a major player, starring in an Academy Award production.

Yuval Noah Harari, "does history have a script? Is history moving relentlessly towards unity? Is your script part of the universal order which governs the entire world?"

Harari, like many individuals, wonders if "all things happen for a reason."

Are we just following our script?

> *Man did not weave the web of life,*
> *He is merely a strand in it*
> *Whatever he does to the web,*
> *He does to himself.*

NATIVE AMERICAN PROVERB

YOU completed your dress rehearsal in the universe.

YOU made your grand entrance at birth.

YOUR final exit occurs when your lines are completed.

YOU enact your brief appearance on the world stage, following your script and timeline.

YOUR life involves many mask and scene transitions.

YOU have numerous entrances and exits.

Deepak Chopra, "in the brain, it takes the coordinated effort of neurons scattered here and yonder to produce the three-dimensional image we call the physical world. This kind of coordination is also instantaneous, just as it is with elementary particles. The entire scheme works as a whole. On a movie set, the director calls for lighting, photography, sound, and action. Each one is a separate setup, and coordinating takes time. But when you look out at the world, the mind does not say, I got the lights going. Where is the sound? Will somebody cue the sound, please? Instead, there is instantaneous coordination of all the elements needed to produce the movie of life."

The movie of life is YOU.

YOU are a star performer in the universal script, playing on the world stage.

YOUR contributions are essential to its success.

GEORGE HARRISON, "THAT WAS THE GREAT THING about John and what I got from him, from all those years. He saw that we are not just in the material world; he saw beyond death, that this life is just a little play that is going on. And he understood that."

Script (Life Journey)

MARK TWAIN, "THE MOST IMPORTANT DAYS OF YOUR life are the day you were born and the day you found out why?"

Your script defines your purpose on the world stage.

Carl Jung, "the future is unconsciously prepared long in advance and therefore can be guessed by clairvoyants."

You entered onto the world stage knowing your purpose, as recorded in your script. A newborn child often has gripped fists at birth. Does this symbolize the infant entering their role on the world stage clutching their script? To us invisible, but to the child it is visible.

You were involved in writing and editing your script, you agreed to your role on the world stage. You knew the other actors, the mask, and the scene changes allocated to you.

From your first scene to your final scene, you are guided by your script, your purpose for this life.

Harari, "the script gives meaning to your words, emotions, and physical gestures. We each have a beginning and an end. We cannot live forever. We all play a role in some great cosmic drama devised by the Gods or by the laws of nature."

Everything that happens in your script is designed to move you, the world stage, and the universe forward in unison. We are ALL evolving.

Christopher Columbus, "following the light of the sun, we left the old world."

The Nazi concentration camps were horror at the extreme. Yet within those walls, many chose an attitude of survival.

David Brook even, "the most miserable conditions cannot upend inner peace."

Perhaps inner peace comes from a 'knowing' and trust in your script.

Our life's purpose becomes visible to us through our performance on the world stage.

Harari, "the purpose to our life becomes clear with time through the role we play."

Many see their purpose as an inner compass.

To others, their purpose is the 'light' of their internal torch guiding them and others on their journey.

Margaret Fuller, "if you have knowledge, let others light their candle in it."

Life coach, Sabine Buhlmann, envisions each of us having our own "inner GPS." Is this our script?

'Time out' is sought when you feel blocked or stuck.

Are these exits a time to re-evaluate, and realign yourself with your script?

Do you make an entrance back onto the world stage to resume your role from your dressing room?

The script, Harari reflects, is a "great cosmic plan."

Perhaps an infinite script is written before our arrival and flows on after our departure.

Harari, "life has a script, playwright, director, producer, and meaning and are orchestrated by the divine presence of the universe."

The script is not random; it has dharma, a purpose.

Harari, "the actors are in a real-life journey. We, as humans, fulfill a role in the great drama. Through divine drama our lives have meaning and purpose."

Your script is your reason for being here and motivation to 'shine like the star' you are each day.

A child's birth begins their role on the world stage.

Harari, "we all signed up on the day we were born."

Each newborn is the new wave from the universe, a blessing to the universal script.

Martin Luther King Jr., "and babies we are told are the latest news from heaven."

Every birth is a new scene in the universal script. Each new scene attempts to improve the world they were born into through evolution.

David Brook, "the world is the stage on which holiness can be achieved."

Our script connects us to other actors and settings.

Harari, "your script gives meaning to your life through your journey into your own inner experiences and then connecting with the meaning of the entire universe."

Synchronicity occurs when your own experiences and the universal script are in harmony with each other.

Harari, "humans enjoy physical and mental health when the inner movements of their body and soul are in harmony with the heavenly music created by the stars."

Pope Gregory the Great, composed the Gregorian chants. He felt the true author of the chants to be the Holy Spirit. Gregory felt he was a conduit, a vessel and that God was the ultimate source of all art, music, literature, and nature's splendor.

An old friend recounted her husband's passing. She wanted to make her husband comfortable and played the Gregorian chants as he faded.

For our own mom, we played the Tibetan Singing Bowls as her final mask ebbed.

Each entry and exit are predetermined. They fit perfectly into the master script.

David Brook, "the main story, is the soul story."

Your entry and exit are pre-ordained and blessed. You are received with love and returned with love.

Harari, "so even the war, plague and drought will work out for the best – if not here and now, then in the afterlife."

Your script is an original, never to be repeated. It is an infinite script. It is timeless. It moves forward on its own timeline.

There are many entrances and exits. Many opportunities for lessons to be learned, all written into your script for its success.

Martin Luther King Jr., "death comes to every individual. There is an amazing democracy about death. It is not an aristocracy for some of the people but a democracy for all of the people. Kings die, and beggars die; rich men die, and poor men die, old people die, and young people die; death comes to the innocent, and it comes to the guilty. Death is the irreducible common denominator of all men. Death is not the end. Death is not a period that ends the great sentence of life but a comma that punctuates it to a more lofty significance. Death is not a blind alley that leads the human race into a state of nothingness, but an open door which leads man into eternal life."

Your next script will begin with your rebirth and the continuation of the infinite script.

The days when you are connected to your script are 'magical'. Life is good. You see sunshine in an overcast day.

Deepak Chopra, "trust that your soul has a plan and even if you can't see it all, know everything will unfold as it is meant to."

It is the same trust that a helpless newborn expresses to their parents. Their parents are everything to the newborn and provide all essential needs for them to survive and thrive.

Each script has a director, your higher self, your soul, who provides the same love and direction parents do for their newborns.

LEONARD COHEN, "THERE IS A CRACK IN EVERY-THING, that's how the light gets in."

SUPPORT FOR YOUR SCRIPT

Dharma

Deepak Chopra perceives dharma as "our life's true purpose."

Your dharma is the source of your script, the invisible guide.

Deepak Chopra, "we are all here for a specific purpose. When you connect with your dharma, you live your life with enthusiasm and passion. Your life with dharma is in harmony with cosmic law."

A seeker seeks their passions and, ultimately, their reason for being here.

Deepak Chopra, "passion is energy. It's the power that comes from focusing on what really excites you."

When following your script, you are free and aligned with your dharma.

Robert Frost, "freedom lies in being bold" and following your passion.

Your script is unique. You are unique, when at one with your script, you live each day in 'joy'.

Deepak Chopra, "when we live with enthusiasm, we fully engage our brains and bodies in our activities. With this enthusiasm, we build new pathways that foster health and well-being. Finding our dharma enables us to serve our community and ourselves in deeply meaningful ways. Engaging in life in this way helps keep our minds active and sharp and strengthens our relationships with everyone we meet. Our dharma is a unique talent, and we will express it in our unique way."

When implementing our dharma in service to others (people, animals, environment), we often ask how can I help?

> *YOUR dharma isn't really about YOU.*
> *It's meant to feel good so you keep doing it,*
> *but really it's about serving humanity and*
> *and raising the vibration of the planet.*

SAHARA ROSE

THE ANSWER TO THIS QUESTION REQUIRES ONE TO diminish the control of their ego.

This allows our true spirit, our higher self, to connect to the universe's infinite knowledge and wisdom.

Deepak Chopra, "connection with dharma ignites our self-awareness and is in step with the cosmos."

Dharma is a 'calling' of our special talents, our special gifts that we brought onto the world stage, with each of us, from the universe. Each gift serves our purpose on the world stage.

Frederick Lenz, "souls have different journeys. The best thing to know is not what everybody else does but what you do. Self-discovery is finding your own dharma, your own rhythm."

Dharma's intention is to expand our awareness and create inner bliss.

Ruben Chavez, "pay attention to the things you are naturally drawn to. They are often connected to your path, passion, and purpose in life. Have the courage to follow them."

One way to access your dharma is through meditation.

> *Your dharma is your divine purpose on this*
> *planet,*
> *your soul's essence,*
> *the unique vibration only YOU can carry out in*
> *the world.*

SAHARA ROSE

Meditation

Deepak Chopra, meditation is "the software of your soul."

Meditation practices are innate in each of us. It is one of our most undervalued gifts from the universe.

We enter through meditation, and we leave through meditation. It is our, 'go to place'.

Thomas Carlyle, "silence is the element in which great things fashion themselves."

Meditation can take place on a walk-in nature, on a run, a swim, on a ski hill, a bike ride, a sail, a walk on the beach, or anywhere where you find 'peace and stillness'.

Michael Singer, "silence is to be quiet or to be still. It is in silence the soul can speak to the attentive listener."

Silence permits a union between the lower self and the higher self.

Ramana Maharshi, "it is the higher power which does everything, and the man is only a fool. If he accepts that position, he is free from troubles."

Is evolution moving us toward the union of the lower self and the higher self?

Ram Dass, "the quieter you become, the more you can hear."

In your quiet time, does your lower self surrender to your higher self?

Each breath has a rhythm, a sweet sound of inhalation and exhalation.

Wolfgang Amadeus Mozart, "the music is not in the notes, but in the silence between."

In the time between an inhale and an exhale, a connection is made to the universe. When in this still space, there is an 'opening'. This opening is pure consciousness, the space where new ideas and thoughts develop.

This opening connects each of us to our script. Your lower and higher self review your next scene and mask change in this space.

Your higher self, your soul, is your director. This is the space of pure intention. The 'magic' is in transitioning the power of the silence back into our busy daily lives.

Deepak Chopra, "in the silence of meditation, we connect with our higher selves, the field of pure potentiality, and plant the seeds of our dearest intentions for ourselves and others so that they flourish in their lives. In this stillness, we come to understand we are indeed intrinsically part of the universe. We feel connected with everybody and everything around us and come to know ourselves as magnificently powerful beings who can manifest anything we desire. Knowing that my actions and desires are supported by cosmic intelligence. Silence connects us with our spirit."

In my early years, prayer was part of my life.

At university, there was a gradual transition to meditation. I took many psychology courses and became curious about mindfulness and living in the present.

By my late 20's, I was meditating most days. I could sometimes feel a 'tingling' in my hands, feelings of connection to something infinite, loving, all forgiving, and comforting.

My meditations grew to be part of my daily practice.

I have developed my own personal ways of connecting to my higher self.

Through trial and error, I have found I connect best through nature. A favorite meditation is when I fade into a vast, old welcoming tree, where I feel at one with ALL.

Meditations can shift you from:
Fear to Love
Ego to Spirit
Separation to Unity.

DEEPAK CHOPRA

DURING MEDITATION, YOU CAN OFTEN MOVE FROM grievances and pain to forgiveness, gratitude, and grace.

In this still space, you sow seeds of intentions into the fertile field of all possibilities. At the appropriate time, they will bloom and flourish in the days, months, and years to come. The events are slow-moving, the journey filled with highs, lows, and moments of 'joy'.

Buddha, "thru who you are" these slow-moving acts create suitable thoughts and actions. Love, tolerance, forgiveness, and non-judgmental virtues help to 'radiate pure being'.

Meditation allows you to participate in the divine dance, the cosmic dance.

Meditation connects you with all visible and invisible angels.

Meditation awakens your dharma, your reason for being here. 'Still time' connects you with your script and gently reminds you of your next lines.

YOU were born with unique gifts
YOU were meant to share with the world.
Don't keep them hidden.
Share YOUR light.

SAHARA ROSE

DEEPAK CHOPRA, "MEDITATION ALLOWS THE POWER within to attract the energy from the universe to support you on your journey."

The meditative state is 'ego free'. You are free of society and all its tentacles.

Deepak Chopra, "quiet inward attention activates natures evolutionary power benefiting everyone and everything."

Still time connects us to our dharma and 'inner chamber'.

In my adolescent years, I enjoyed spending time with younger children. I babysat and was a playground leader. I was happiest with children.

Danti Alighieri, "three things remain with us from paradise: stars, flowers, and children."

I pursued this, and became a classroom teacher, mother, nain (Welsh for grandmother), and traveling helper. All with a passion and an open heart for young, innocent children. I identify best with souls who have the same heart as me.

On my first trip to India, two Indian friends accompanied me to a hospice for disabled women. On the way, these two beautiful, caring souls recounted how they had become aware of a young disabled mother whose daughter had been taken from her.

The young disabled mother was married to a man who drank and had sold their infant daughter for a few hundred rupees.

My friends rescued the distraught mother and sought out her little girl. The mother was in despair; after several months of searching, my friends were able to reconnect the two, mother and daughter.

They were now living together.

I remember walking down a narrow lane in a poor area of Chennai. I entered and saw a straw floor in a dimly lit room. I met the mother; she dragged herself along the straw floor to greet us. She introduced us to her eighteen-month-old daughter—a bright-eyed, active, healthy little girl.

Few could live in these conditions and be so happy.

It was a HUGE powerful moment for me. My script had brought me to this scene. The love between mother and child was unconditional.

I tried to describe this bottomless love between a young disabled mother and her rescued daughter, but the words never came.

In my meditation, I felt the invisible words and forgiveness for the child's father.

When you talk,
You are only repeating what you already know.
But if you listen,
You may learn something new.

THE DALAI LAMA

Faith

EINSTEIN, "HUMAN BEINGS, VEGETABLES, OR COSMIC dust, we all dance to a mysterious tune, intoned in the distance by an invisible player."

Faith is the connection to the "invisible player."

Jen Sincero, "when you do things from your soul, you feel a river moving in you, a joy. Faith shifts your focus off the past, your old ways of doing things and opens you up to new opportunities, new hows that will create a new reality."

A few years ago, I visited my youngest son in Australia. He lived in Burleigh Heads. It is a small village south of the Gold Coast. It is about an hour train ride to Brisbane. Burleigh Heads is a peaceful place. Every morning, I rose before sunrise and went to Burleigh Beach to watch the sun-up and the early morning surfers. Afterward, I would walk Burleigh Hill, originally an Aboriginal site.

Burleigh Hill is a good hour trek. You follow a meandering path, wild turkeys are in abundance, and lizards of all sizes, and snakes frequent the trail. This walk became part of my daily routine.

One day as I descended Burleigh Hill, I noticed a lady about my age slowly walking in front. She stopped, and as I was about to pass her, I noticed she was observing some birds. A conversation began between us, which is natural for me.

A little while later, a third woman joined us. I felt her vibration first and then noticed her from the corner of my eye. She was young, in a design flowing skirt, barefooted, and wore a straw sun hat over her long, wavy hair.

She stopped to watch the birds with us. She seemed comfortable with us, the two strangers she had just bumped into. She told us, "this is not a chance encounter, I have something to share with you, follow me." Which we did. Imagine following a stranger into the unknown. It was like being in a daydream.

We went off the path, in and out, up and down. She finally stopped. She had brought us to an area I had passed many times, unaware of the significance of this sacred space.

She told us this had been the area where Aboriginal women came to give birth, like our maternity wards. It was an area for women only. She showed us the rocks and trees where the women would lean and how they would position their bodies to give birth. Her description was so real; you could almost hear and feel the women many years ago.

We lingered for a few minutes, each lost in our own thoughts. The younger woman left with a wave, she just faded into the background. The other woman and I chatted for a few minutes; interestingly, she, too, lived in Canada. We each continued our journey.

Burleigh Heads is a small place, but I never saw either of these two women again.

I returned to the beach, walked, and reflected on this experience. I felt so comfortable with these two strangers; it was like revisiting a place the three of us had been together long ago.

Jen Sincero, "an epiphany is a visceral understanding of something you already know."

The timing of bumping into someone and the sharing of energy, that feeling of WOW that was meant to be, is sometimes passed off as a 'coincidence', but is it?

There is an internal knowing of when you are physically and mentally in the right place at the right time. Faith is a special ingredient that is intrinsic in each of us. We were born with faith, and we leave with faith.

Jen Sincero, "faith is a muscle. The more you use it, the stronger it gets."

To nurture faith requires confidence, patience, and listening to your intuition.

On another trip to Australia, I visited the Blue Mountains. My son and I were staying in Sydney, and we had booked an early train ride to the Blue Mountains.

My son had been out with friends the night before and returned late. He slept most of the way on the train. I had wanted to go to the Blue Mountains for many reasons, one being that a good friend's son passed there. I did not know where, just the Blue Mountains.

As the train started making more frequent stops, my son came to life. "Where should we get off?" he asked. I looked at the map on the wall of the train. The name Katoomba resonated with me. I answered, "Katoomba."

Henry David Thoreau, "we must walk consciously only part way toward our goal and then leap in the dark to our success."

We took that leap of faith.

We walked, found a nice place to have breakfast, talked with the locals, and decided to trust ourselves with the day.

In one of the conversations, it was mentioned that the Blue Mountains were a popular spot for young people, but sadly, some passed there. Our first sign!

We visited the Three Sisters at Echo Point, beautiful, majestic natural structures that set the mood. Serendipitously, we followed a welcoming path. We could hear a waterfall in the distance. At one point, the path narrowed, and there was a branch of a tree overhanging the path. On the branch was perched the most beautiful, multi-colored bird, singing away. We paused to really appreciate this scene. Another sign!

As we walked by the tree, branch, and bird, along the path I kept gazing back at the bird. I remember thinking I will reflect on this later, which I did. As we came off the path and headed back to the train, I saw several vans that young people had turned into homes for their travels. Another sign!

I put those three signs into a compartment in my head, to reflect on later.

Jen Sincero, "have faith you and the universe have created everything for your growth and be grateful for it."

When I returned home, I spoke with my friend whose son had passed in the Blue Mountains. She wanted to know if I had visited the Blue Mountains. "Yes", I replied. "Where did you go?" I answered, "Katoomba." There was silence, and then a soft voice replied, "that is where her son left from". His mother later confirmed that her son's parked van was found in the area.

Later, when I reflected on that day, I thanked the universe for the day. For allowing me to see where my friend's son departed from and to feel his last scenes.

Being confident in your internal compass, waiting patiently for your new reality to come forth requires patience and faith.

Upon reflection, I had faith that the bird was connected to my friend's son. Witnessing the vans was how he had lived. My 'faith' had given me the privilege of walking in his footsteps.

Being positive and seeing everyone and everything in your day as a teacher helps to make each second of your day exciting and refreshing.

Jen Sincero, "treading water in your comfort zone is a yawn/snore."

Faith is opening the door, leaving the safety of your home, and walking out into the unknown, to see what life has to offer you. Faith allows you to be a risk taker.

An ancient Indian proverb, "certain things catch your eye, but pursue only those that capture the heart."

Faith is believing in your inner light to guide you, wherever your vibration is most needed.

An old Arabic proverb, "close the door that brings the wind and relax."

Faith bestows confidence to wait out any storm.

> *I worked for a menial's hire,*
> *Only to learn, dismayed*
> *That any wage I asked of life*
> *Life would have willingly paid.*

ANONYMOUS

WE LEARN, THROUGH OUR MANY EXPERIENCES, TO have faith in our inner voice.

Deepak Chopra, "having faith that all answers lie within and all we have to do is to listen to the inner song of truth."

With faith comes an unfolding of life both inside and out, which is in harmony with the universal script.

When I was in Uganda, I visited a local 'witch doctor' in the Bwindi area. He was a colorful gentleman. He believed in natures medicines and, after listening patiently to a villager, would offer local plants to heal physical and mental issues.

I watched and could feel the villagers faith in the witch doctor and his natural therapies.

SAINT AUGUSTINE, "FAITH IS TO BELIEVE WHAT YOU do not see. The reward of this faith is to see what you believe."

Optimism and Forgiveness

DEEPAK CHOPRA, "OPTIMISM ALLOWS US TO REACH higher and to be at ONE with our higher self. Eat right for your body, meditate daily, exercise, and allow positive thoughts to nourish our lifestyle. Our goal is to be healthy and strong for the rest of our lives.

> *I believe,*
> *I trust,*
> *I let go."*

Every mask, every scene, and every experience is best served with optimism.

Anne Frank, "how wonderful it is that nobody need wait a single moment before starting to improve the world."

Being aware that each positive action and thought in the present moment can lead to a better world is exhilarating.

Bill McNabb, "when you have setbacks and failures, you can overreact to them. You need to step back, analyze them, and learn from them. But you also need to stay optimistic."

I was once a working mom, balancing many mask and scene changes in a day.

I had many invisible and visible angels as cheerleaders and guides. I was so grateful for their support; I was always saying thank you. I acknowledged with each thank you and feeling of optimism that I was allowing grace to enter, linger, and help me have a successful day.

As a working parent, most of my mask transitions began in my mode of transportation, for the day. Whether on foot, bike, or in a car, I could feel the shift.

I would leave our home and allow the mom mask to fade. As I approached the school where I taught, I could sense the teaching mask transitioning on. My teaching mask involved many daily roles: teacher, friend to students and colleagues, social worker, disciplinarian, humanitarian, judge, etc.

On the way home, more mask changes: mother, wife, and daughter. I recall my teaching mask fading. I would knowingly prepare for my new mask, which would serve me well for the rest of my day.

I was slowly evolving with the understanding of not allowing a dark moment to decay the day for myself and others.

Mata Amritanandamayi, "if we dive deep into ourselves, we will find the one thread of universal love that ties all beings together."

Each deserving child I met in developing countries, I met with optimism.

I was fully aware that their life was not, and would probably not, be an easy life. I honored each of their roles on the world stage.

Deepak Chopra, "through optimism, one can watch one's life unfold in divine ways."

I have learned after many disappointments that forgiveness of self and others is an optimistic door to enter.

A global news story that tweaked my quest for understanding optimism and forgiveness in life was presented on 60 Minutes some years ago. It was a true story that occurred in the 1994 Rwanda genocide.

A man and woman from Rwanda were being interviewed. They had lived side by side in rural Rwanda. The male neighbor had killed many members of the female neighbor's family during the genocide.

While the man was in prison, he wrote to his female neighbor and asked for her forgiveness.

When he was released from prison, they became friends. I watched this, and it was an 'awe' moment.

Deepak Chopra, "we are always learning. Be open so lessons can be mastered. Forgive yourself and others and move on."

There are moments throughout each of our days when 'stuff' happens.

Abraham Lincoln's words have carried me far over the years, "we can complain because rose bushes have thorns, or rejoice because thorn bushes have roses."

I am in a sensitive temple, my body. My sensitivity has been my best friend and, at times, my thorn.

I know when my sensitivity is moving toward a mask I no longer want to wear. I am grateful to have acquired the tools to recognize this negativity.

During these darker times, I attempt to bring 'light' in and move into a more positive mindset.

Munia Khan, "the light within us can always identify our mind's darkness."

I like to think of each day as an 'outward bound' adventure. When I walk out the door in the morning, no matter where I am, I feel I am leaving the safety of my harbor and heading for open seas, the unknown.

Angela Duckworth, "this optimism allows tenacity to enter and an undefeatable spirit to rise."

When your optimism mask begins to feel secure, you are guided by the light of the universe into a safe harbor.

SUSAN J BISSONETTE, "AN OPTIMIST IS THE HUMAN personification of spring."

Surrender

MICHAEL SINGER, "SURRENDER TEACHES YOU TO honor the transformative power of life deeply. Your desire to be steered into calmer waters, for stillness, for clarity and chatter to cease. Letting go of one's self-centered thoughts and emotions was all that was needed for profound, professional, and spiritual growth."

I see two selves in my body.

One is my lower self, my ego self, who is forever chatting. The chatter is mostly negative babble, thoughts, and reasons to stay put.

The other is my higher self, my universal director, my soul. My higher self is silent and communicates through intuition, senses, and nature.

My higher self ushers me to signs in my day. These markers guide me to my scenes and teachers who escort me through my lessons.

In Michael Singer's words, surrendering your lower self permits your higher self to use its "invisible hand of life" to shepherd you on your way.

As I have aged, there is now supreme trust in my higher self. The hourglass of my life continues to show me I have less time in front and still much to do.

Meditation, movement, and nature all support me, quieting my lower self's voice and turning off the negative chatter.

Eckhart Tolle, "in surrender, you no longer need ego defenses and false masks."

Being at one with my higher self, my soul, releases feelings of loneliness and darkness.

Mother Teresa called these dark times "dark nights that all spiritual masters must endure."

Mother Teresa, in her service to the poor, the 'untouchables' witnessed first-hand their feelings of being undesired.

She also witnessed the indomitable strength of their soul to pursue their journey. Mother Teresa was in the trenches with the souls she identified most with on her own personal spiritual journey.

Mastin Kipp, "surrender and accept that whatever is happening in the moment, the universe is working on your behalf."

Being in union with one's higher self allows hope to enter. Hope fosters change to manifest itself for a better day to unfold for each of us.

When you connect with your higher self, you are in the realm of your spirit and infinite possibilities. This space is where miracles are created. The veil between this dimension and the next room in the universe is at its finest.

Deepak Chopra, "deep down, you know the enlightenment you seek is worth the temporary discomfort of the journey."

Enlightenment involves 'expanding beyond thought'.

I have my moments of doubt, days when I am stuck, days when I give in. Days when I unknowingly permit my lower self to chat.

As I age, I can mostly recognize the retreat to my lower self.

How do I handle this? I ask for HELP. During the day, when I can feel myself slipping and almost every night before I drift off, I ask for 'help'.

Rumi, "life is a balance of holding on and letting go."

I often think of souls who have/are experiencing extreme physical and mental abuse. Do they move to the passenger side and permit their higher self to handle their horrific situation?

Do you give permission for your higher self to rescue you?

Michael Singer, "surrendering to life was my path to realization."

Michael Singer feels surrendering to the "flow of life" connects us to ALL and to infinite possibilities.

Surrendering illuminates your script.

MARK NEPO, "SURRENDER IS LIKE A FISH FINDING the current and going with it."

Breath

Thich Nhat Hanh, "feelings come and go like clouds in a windy sky. Conscious breathing is my anchor."

Each breath is a gift. Generally, we are not aware we are even breathing.

The occasional cold, where we become congested, makes us aware of our breath. My dad had emphysema, and his illness emphasized the 'gift' of a breath.

Deepak Chopra explains that everything alive is energized by a force called 'prana'. "Prana means energy of life force, and in humans, that life force is breath."

I became attuned to my breath during my 'still time' and my yoga practice.

I like to keep my life simple.

For my meditation, I focus on my breath.

I breathe in on So and breathe out with Hum. I breathe slowly in and out while mentally repeating my So Hum mantra.

My 'still time' can be while quietly sitting or moving. Working with my breath brings clarity, balance, and often new thoughts.

New 'ways', new eyes to look at a scene that is causing discomfort.

Deepak Chopra, "breath bathes our brain and every cell in our body in energy and vitality."

When focusing on your breath, you are in the NOW. Eckhart Tolle believes the NOW is the only absolute moment.

In the NOW, it is possible to raise your vibrational frequency, improve your natural self-healing capability, slow down the aging process, and strengthen your immune system.

When you consciously move with it, your breath can shift your frame of mind from negative to positive.

The more you practice with your breath, the more your inner and outer awareness will expand.

Conscious breathing can transition you from your lower self to your higher self. The gap between each breath is your maskless zone. For that brief interlude you are connected to your script, your director, and all your invisible angels.

. . .

EACH BREATH CONNECTS YOU TO THE NATURAL rhythm of the universe. You witness this at the seashore:

> waves rolling in (inhale)
>
> waves receding (exhale)

You inhale wisdom and light from your script and exhale darkness and negative thoughts.

Each breath is life,

The absence of breath is the absence of life.

Simple. Just breathe.

RUMI, "THE SOUL LIVES THERE IN THE SILENT breath."

Senses

Bill Bryson, "we interpret our world through our senses."

Our senses ground us in this dimension and support our health and growth. Each sense is a fine-tuned antenna. Our senses connect us to the NOW.

Eckhart Tolle, "use your senses fully and let the alert stillness within you be the perceiver, rather than your mind."

Bill Bryson believes we have 33 senses, each 'knowing' where and how we are doing.

New York Times, "a sense may be defined as a mechanism which allows a human or animal to receive special information about the world."

Each day is a new scene for your senses. The projector behind your eyes runs all the potential scenes for your new day.

Marcel Proust, "the real voyage of discovery consists not in seeking new lands but seeing with new eyes."

You choose through 'free will' the scene you want to be in with guidance from your intuition and senses.

Your intuition is your higher self, the director of your script.

A decision as simple as a walk involves the choice between many different scenes. You choose the best walk, knowing intuitively the potential of bumping into someone or touching, smelling, hearing, seeing, or tasting that which could raise your vibration for the day.

Eckhart Tolle, "when you appreciate something simple – a sound, a sight, a touch – when you see beauty, when you feel loving kindness toward another, sense the inner spaciousness that is the source and background to that experience."

Your senses will guide you on the walk.

It becomes a delightful 'sensory experience', how your walk will enhance your day and enrich you as a person.

Wherever I am, when I head out for a walk or bike ride, I always have a general sense of my route. But 'things' change. I am open to the new scenes that appear—trusting that 'it was meant to be'.

You become receptive to the gentle winds of the universe. You trust the peaceful breeze to steer you to a 'welcoming' path.

I become energized when a new pathway 'opens up' and have faith all my senses will guide me.

W.B. Yeats, "the world is full of magic things, patiently waiting for our senses to grow sharper."

Our many senses help to guide us through our day.

. . .

BILL BRYSON FEELS THAT OUR SENSES "INTERPRET" the world for us:

A strange smell alerts or brings us pleasure.

Seeing and hearing rushing water warns or beckons us to see its beauty.

Touching can be gentle or harsh.

Eyes take in beauty and signs of danger.

Our senses are our guides.

Each sense is a support for a day filled with infinite possibilities.

IMMANUEL KANT, "ALL OUR KNOWLEDGE BEGINS with our senses."

Emotions

MAYA ANGELOU, "I'VE LEARNED THAT PEOPLE WILL forget what you said, people will forget what you did, but people will never forget how you made them feel."

When helping children in developing countries, I am aware I do not speak their language; I cannot remember every child I see. But I do remember 'feelings' of hope from each deserving child.

My father was born in Wales. I have relatives who still live there. When I visit, I have this feeling of returning home. Life is simple in North Wales. There are few people, mostly nature and castles.

A few years back, I spoke with my uncle about feelings of longing; I had to return to Wales. He said there was a Welsh word for this feeling: 'hiraeth'.

BBC website, "hiraeth is a blend of homesickness, nostalgia, and longing. Hiraeth is a pull on the heart that conveys a distinct feeling of missing something irretrievably lost."

As always, I thanked the universe for setting my course. I laced up my shoes and went for a walk.

During my walk, I reflected that I was about 65 when the feelings of hiraeth visited me. I was officially a senior. I prefer to use the word 'elder'.

I was beginning to experience a longing to return home, but which home? England, where I was born, or my return to the universe.

I slowly understood that a return to the universe was connecting with my higher self.

Angela Duckworth "when negativity bubbles up – think about it and use it."

When negativity visits, see it as a signpost. What can you learn from this scene?

Practice changing a negative emotion into a positive emotion. Celebrate your positives and learn from your negatives. Be proud of who you are.

Make a conscious effort to find the positive in every scene. This approach will promote your recovery from your setbacks while gaining valuable wisdom in the process.

Angela Duckworth, "use mistakes and problems to get better – not reasons to quit."

As a classroom teacher, I had many 'wash out' lessons. I often realized I was losing my student's attention and quickly re-adjusted my lesson plan to suit the day and mood of the class. This skill took many years of teaching to acquire and many moments of introspection.

I soon realized it was my problem. I learned to 'read' my class and would postpone a lesson until the time was right or adjust the delivery of the lesson to suit the 'vibes' of the class. Both teaching strategies came after much reflection, patience, and wanting only the best for each of my students.

Many times in my teaching career, I questioned who was the teacher, me or my students?

Angela Duckworth, "our opponent creates challenges that help us become our best selves."

On most teaching days, I learned more from my students than they acquired from me.

One special student stood out. He had severe asthma and missed many days of school. But when he was in attendance, no one worked harder than this young student. I learned so much from his self-discipline and work ethic.

Many years later, his mother called me to say he had passed. She knew I had named one of my sons after her son. She wanted me to know. Many emotions rushed through me with this sad news.

Throughout your day, you feel many sensations. Some days are like a roller coaster, but your successes and non-successes are all lessons.

The emotions that are attached to these feelings are markers. They guide you to possible readjustment of your sails on your journey.

Harari, "emotions are biochemical algorithms that are vital for the survival and reproduction of all animals."

Emotions support our evolution, mask, and scene changes.

WINSTON CHURCHILL, "SUCCESS CONSISTS OF GOING from failure to failure without loss of enthusiasm."

Love

Wordsworth, "what we have loved, others will love, and we will teach them how."

I see my role now as an elder and a channel for the universe. I only desire to be a conduit for the vibration of love, pure white light. Love's light, with time, will diminish darkness.

> *Darkness cannot drive out darkness;*
> *only light can do that.*
> *Hate cannot drive out hate;*
> *only LOVE can do that.*
>
> Martin Luther King Jr.

When I am in developing countries, I have no words for the unfairness and hardships I see.

On my first visit to India, my friend said to me, "open your hands wider," when I was helping children.

I did; sometimes, I could feel a gentle energy flow from my hands. I internally asked that the energy go wherever and to whomever, it was needed. I trusted the universe to guide its light.

Edith Wharton, "there are two ways of spreading light, to be the candle or the mirror that reflects it."

Love is the highest vibration in the universe and can heal and solve most issues.

During my visit to Chennai, I had connected with two enlightened women. One day they picked me up early and took me to a white catholic church in a poor area of Chennai.

We entered the doors of the church. In the vestibule, we saw two aging nuns. They were each sitting on a worn, wooden stool. I felt love immediately for these two seasoned souls.

They were sitting with their rosary beads, deep in prayer. We stood and waited with reverence.

Eventually, they both looked up; one of the nuns looked at me and, with a strong French accent, said, "where have you been?"

I instinctively knew we had been together in another life. There was just this strong understanding, this 'knowing'.

These two precious souls then took us to the side of the church. There was a makeshift building, which we entered. It reminded me of a manger scene.

We walked slowly through, and everywhere we saw fading humans lying on clean, fresh straw. Most in tattered clothing, most lying in the fetal position. Most elderly.

There was love everywhere I turned. I was told these were the lucky ones. The sisters and their helpers would walk through Chennai's streets in the early morning hours with an old, worn wooden cart. They would assist poor souls close to death onto their cart.

The two loving nuns would bring them back to this hospice shelter and give them dignity in their last scene, their last mask change. Love was given and received among these souls.

I could see and feel the love in this humble final dwelling for so many souls. They were treated with respect, each blessed with an acknowledgment of a life well lived.

Willa Carter, "where there is great love, there are always miracles."

I saw Willa's miracles in these two elderly nuns. The love they had for humanity was their gift, which they gave to ALL.

On another trip to India, we visited a leprosy hospice. The women and men were in separate areas. When we visited the men's residence, they were all primarily busy with projects. Many of the men were involved with a printing press that had been given to them in the 1950s by a Rotary Club in Chatham, Ontario. I live in Ontario and know of Chatham. Another 'awe' moment.

The women were mostly idle. No projects, sitting and struggling to move.

I found this difficult and wondered how I could help.

I went for a brief walk around their dwellings, turned a corner, and saw a garbage heap. In the center was a beautiful lime tree. It was lush and bearing small green limes: unbelievable, in a garbage heap!

Deepak Chopra, "love is like gifts waiting to be opened."

I felt this instant connection to the lime tree. I talked to some friends and arranged for the garbage heap to be turned into a garden for the leprosy women. Now they too, would have a purposeful day.

Love conquers all hostility and negativity. It is the true essence of our being.

Love allows the unlimited possibilities of the universe to open its many radiant doors for you.

Walk with love in your being, and share its light wherever you sail.

MARIANNE WILLIAMSON, "THE SPIRITUAL JOURNEY IS the unlearning of fear and the acceptance of LOVE."

Food and Water

HIPPOCRATES, "LET FOOD BE THY MEDICINE AND medicine be thy food."

Perfect words, I listen to my body, and my body guides me to make good healthy food choices that are right for me.

Deepak Chopra, "choose food that helps you thrive."

I am a vegetarian; my staples are fruits, grains, vegetables, lentils, and water.

Deepak Chopra, "as conscious breathing invites greater prana, so do nutritious food and fresh, clean water. We trust the inner wisdom of our bodies to guide us to the right food choices."

Deepak continues, "it is important to make food choices that are in tune with your body and eat with awareness to stay healthy and to thrive. Eating an array of colorful foods rich in nutrients and pleasing to the eye in a calming setting sets the mood for a healthy environment. Being aware of the six tastes: sweet, sour, salty, bitter, pungent, and astringent and trying to incorporate them into your meals helps to align our doshas and to keep us balanced. Eating for balance is achieved by choosing food that is in harmony with our unique bodies and our unique needs. Listening to our bodies, we can choose the best food that helps us feel balanced, energized, vital, and whole. Try to include sight, taste, smell, and color in each meal."

When I deviate from a well-balanced diet, I do not like the consequences and quickly return to healthy food choices.

Benjamin Franklin, "to lengthen thy life, lessen thy meals."

Our body is our temple. It is up to us and our choices to nourish our bodies so that they can be at peak performance each day for us.

It is our vessel for this lifetime, respect it, listen to it, and thank it daily.

I have witnessed children, animals, and adults who suffer from malnutrition.

I have witnessed children and adults who, due to unclean water, have been born with or developed river blindness.

I honor these souls, their vibrations, and their role on our world stage.

BILL BRYSON, "YOUR BODY IS YOUR LONG-SUFFERING servant."

Angels

BERNIE SIEGAL, "GOD SENDS US MANY ANGELS IN many forms to awaken us and guide us on the path we are meant to live."

I believe we all have angels, both visible and invisible.

Angels are pure love and stay with us through good and dire times. They know our script, each scene and mask change, and our dharma for this life.

They are our support actors. They will move mountains for our success. Angels are our cheerleaders and comforters.

James Russell Lowell, "all God's angels come to us disguised."

Over my 70 years, I have had numerous dogs. Each one an angel to me. They were always there for me. Numerous teachers, friends, trees, sunsets, sunrises, and strangers have been my angels.

I can feel my angel's presence in my dark times, trying to turn the light on, for me.

WASTELAND

Who is the third who walks always with you?
When I count thee are only you and I together
But when I look ahead up the white road
There is always another one walking beside you
Gliding wrapt in a brown mantle, hooded
I do not know whether a man or a woman
But who is that on the other side of you?

T.S. ELLIOTT

I RECALL VISITING A FRIEND IN MAINE. MY HUSBAND and I drove for our friend's mother's funeral. We rowed out to her family island. We sat on her family's front porch, looking out to the water.

We watched two massive eagles fly in front of us. They settled on a nearby tree's branches by the water. I intuitively knew they were connected to my friend's deceased parents. Each coming to reassure my friend that 'all is well'.

My angels, I feel most when I have my darkest thoughts and scenes. I can feel their encouraging words, "just keep moving forward."

Angela Duckworth, "it feels we have nothing left to give, and yet, in those dark and desperate moments, we find that if we just keep putting one foot in front of the other, there is a way to accomplish what all reason seems to argue against."

As an educator, I witnessed many students who had disabilities, but who never let their disabilities handicap them.

I could feel their angels, and sometimes I felt their unseen hands and unheard voices guiding the child's assistants and me to do what was best for the child.

There was a connection, which I treasured. We worked as a united team. We all wanted our 'magic' to move the child forward, to be the best they could be in this life.

PROVERB, "ANGELS SPEAK TO THOSE WHO SILENCE their minds long enough to hear."

Hope

Hope is the thing with feathers
That perches in the soul,
And sings the tune without the words,
And never stops at all

EMILY DICKENSON

HOPE IS A MASK WE ALL WEAR WHEN WANTING OR experiencing change.

Hope releases us from negativity and gives us the strength to move on.

Omar M Al-Aqeel, "the wings of angels are hope and faith."

Hope initiates positive feelings within each of us.

Sometimes when helping children in developing countries, I talk to a random child and their parents. A translator is present. I often begin with prepared questions but depending on time and comfort, I sometimes go off script.

I recall meeting a young girl and her mother outside her rural school. It was an extremely poor area; each child was given lunch, and many street children were just wandering about.

Desmond Tutu, "hope is being able to see that there is light despite all of the darkness."

I asked the deserving young girl about her school. She replied, "she liked school." Her mother very proudly added she was "good at school." I then asked, "what would you like to be when you grow up."

Her eyes lit up, "a mother". She continued, "she wanted to be like her mother."

Her own mother gave me a look. I interpreted that look to mean, please give her hope for a different life. I gingerly replied, "because she liked school and because she was doing well at school, maybe she could dream of being a teacher."

That little girl now had the same look as her mother had. I believe it was a look of hope.

Robert Browning, "I hold that a man should strive to the utmost for his life's set prize."

Our life script was written with the pen of hope.

Every individual is constantly striving to be the best they can be. Hope is our wings to achieve what we may believe to be the impossible.

Hope emboldens us and asks nothing of us in return.

I end my day each night, hoping for my lessons to appear the next day. I hope the tools to master my lessons will surface from within me.

I awake each morning with hope for a good day.

Elizabeth Barrett Browning, "light tomorrow with today."

When visiting the leprosy hospice mentioned earlier, there was a woman who I connected with. She had beautiful gray hair swept up onto her head. Her face was disfigured due to leprosy, but to me, she was stunning. She wore a simple blue sari, matching her blue eyes.

There was a bond and hope in her face that things might be different. I hope the garden was her answer.

LAILAH GIFTY AKITA, "HOPE IS A BELIEF IN A BETTER tomorrow."

Grace

Deepak Chopra, "GRACE IS THE AMOUNT OF LIGHT in our soul."

When traveling in India and Nepal, the common greeting is to put your hands together, about chest level, bow slightly, and say, "Namaste." This greeting spoke to me immediately.

I liked the thought of my inner light greeting your inner light. I internalized this greeting to be one of reverence and respect.

There are spaces when one is experiencing change, when your mask is fading, and a new scene is materializing.

Simone Weil sees those spaces as opportunities for grace to enter. "Grace fills empty spaces, but it can only enter where there is a void to receive it, and it is grace itself which makes this void."

By saying yes to life, grace slowly moves into the spaces and fills the openings with light. Optimism spills over, and a sense of being in the right place at the right time visits you and wants to stay.

Eckhart Toile, "say yes to life and see how life starts working with you instead of against you."

Our individual script keeps order in our life. It is our timeline. It encourages us to say YES to life.

Isaac Newton, "nothing in life is happening out of order."

Grace appears throughout each of our lives. Grace surfaces when it is time to adjust our sails. To move into our new scene and to transition to our new mask.

John Newton, "Amazing grace! How sweet the sound that saved a wretch like me! I once was lost but now am found, was blind but now I see."

Grace visited me when I retired from teaching and became a traveling helper. Grace shone its light on all the connectors in my life. Grace allowed me to take an inventory of my journey.

Pierre Teilhard De Chardin, "the universe as we know it is a joint product of the observer and the observed."

I have always considered myself to be an observer of life.

Through grace, I was beginning to see my script, all the scenes, masks, support actors, director, and stage supporting my life's dharma. As my openness expanded, grace visited me often. As I became less rigid, said yes to life, and became more flexible to the dance of my day, I began seeing with different eyes.

Deepak Chopra, "being carefree signals the universe that you trust the universe."

By being carefree, I was trusting the universe and my script to, in Deepak Chopra's words, "manifest through grace," my new world.

With my expansion came some doubt. It was not all bliss. Questions arose inside and outside of me. Eyebrows were raised, and at times my silence grew, but inside there was a 'knowing' that a change in course was necessary, a readjustment of my sails.

Deepak Chopra, "trust in grace through expanded awareness."

I cherish all scene and mask changes thus far in my 70+ years. I cherish my body, my temple for allowing me the strength, energy, and openness to greet most days with joy. I cherish my DNA and all my lives for my faith in my infinite script.

ANNE LAMOTT, "I DO NOT UNDERSTAND THE mystery of grace, only that it meets us where we are, but does not leave us where it found us."

Stage

Mike Dooley, "you crafted the stage you are now on."

Each new day begins with your entrance. You awake with the sunrise. Your stage curtain slowly rises to welcome your brand-new day and the new you.

Maya Angelou, "this is a wonderful day. I've never seen this one before."

The last scene of the day comes with the sunset and your stage curtain lowering on the final scenes of your day. You exit your day to your sleep, where you prepare for your unique tomorrow.

You designed each scene and mask change, each time out, each entrance and exit, each movement forward, and each awareness expansion. All to ensure your dharma, found in your script, would lead to a successful performance on the world stage.

The stage varies each day. It may be one scene or many scenes according to your script.

I recall visiting the Cellular Jail near Port Blair in the Andamans.

The Andaman and Nicobar Islands consist of about 300 Indian islands in the Bay of Bengal. Indigenous islanders inhabit the more remote islands.

The day involved a variety of scenes. We had helped deserving children earlier in the day. Some children had traveled by water and land for four long, uncomfortable, exhausting hours.

Later in the day, we visited the Cellular Jail, which was very disturbing. The British built the Cellular Jail in 1896 for exiled Indian political prisoners.

In a single day, we went from the 'light' of the Andaman children to the 'dark' of the Cellular Jail.

I attempt to educate myself on the area's history, wherever I am. With this knowledge comes an understanding of the evolution of the universal script and the world stage. I try to be 'open' and to appreciate the historical setting at the time and the decisions rendered.

> *On the stage on which we are observing it,*
> *Universal History*
> *Spirit displays itself*
> *In its most concrete reality.*

GEORG WILHELM FRIEDRICH HEGEL

Nelson Mandela, "education is the most powerful weapon which you can use to change the world."

Your early years are spent in a formal school setting.

David Brook, "a school can transform a life."

In high school, I had two teachers who transformed my life, although I did not know it at the time.

One was my English teacher. She introduced the class to Shakespeare's, All The World's A Stage. Her interpretation of this play planted the seeds many years ago for this book.

The second teacher who launched me on my course was my biology teacher. He often imparted to the class that "energy can neither be created nor destroyed." Those powerful words tweaked my curiosity.

Each scene in the school setting was designed for success by you, the student.

Even the 'dark times' were necessary for your growth and the mastery of your lessons.

Schools, in all forms, have been acknowledged throughout human history.

"I make honorable things pleasant to children," wrote a Spartan Educator.

David Brook deems schools to be "information rich." Skilled teaching is comparable to a gardener planting seeds. These seeds will germinate and grow throughout your life. At some point, you will harvest them.

An 'aware' teacher intuitively knows that their students are, in Fred Rogers's words, "closer to God than the adult."

All the different settings for your ever-changing stage are recorded in your script. Each setting designed to enrich your life experience. Each scene, each mask change, embraces opportunities for soul expansion.

Elizabeth Hay, "it was in jail, she said where she became part of a native healing circle. And that changed everything. That is when I gave up my life of blaming. You claim your mistakes. You claim your good qualities, and you do not get stuck. You move around the wheel of life from one level to the next, from the emotional level to the spiritual, making room as you move from something else to center."

We choose settings where the vibration calls you.

Elizabeth Hay, "we are made up of invisible currents."

An intention in this life is to raise our vibration and the vibration of the world stage. You have incorporated, into your script, scenes where potential settings and people will facilitate this to happen. These settings have higher vibrations and wafer-thin veils.

Elizabeth Hay, "thin places where we're closer to the unseen world."

Highly evolved souls, sometimes called 'old souls', enlightened souls, or as Elizabeth Hay calls them, "mystics are drawn to emptiness, a silence as the necessary pre-conditions for an upwelling of the spirit."

Each setting varies as you progress on your life journey. Perhaps you are seeking a vibration with easier access to your script.

Elizabeth Hay, "an electrical connection can create a union between your intuitive side and your rational side."

Aboriginals often choose settings where they are connected to the earth. They prefer, as Elizabeth Hay writes, "make-shift shelters where they are storm-tossed and sun-warmed thru life."

We witnessed this at the Jarawa reserve. Jarawa are indigenous people of the Andaman Islands. It is believed they have inhabited this area for thousands of years. The Jarawa rely entirely on the forest and marine resources for survival.

We saw a young male Jarawa, scantily dressed, walking through the dense underbrush with a hand-made spear. It was our 'joy' to visit his natural world and to connect with its vibration.

Some souls stay put and enjoy the fruits of their environment. Other souls are nomadic and wander the planet breathing in each new place and pursuing its 'magic'. Each choice originated in the universe, nurtured through nature and all the other elements you wrote into your script.

"Each individual is a singular ray of light," proclaims Harari "when each ray is put together, it forms a beautiful rainbow that is visible for many. Some just feel it. It expands and compresses according to the actions and vibrations of the planet."

This connection can elevate the vibration of the world stage. Each of our unique gifts, which accompanied each of us from the universe, has this potential to raise the world stage's vibration.

Every individual actor is special and chooses the appropriate setting for their specialness to radiate.

Socrates, "to know thyself is the beginning of wisdom."

Everyone possesses a distinctive inner voice. You can access your inner voice through connectors such as meditation, prayer, movement, and nature.

Deepak Chopra, "everything I desire is within me."

The inner voice is your wisdom. The inner voice knows your purpose, script, and performing stage. The inner voice knows the reason for your life and works in harmony with the universe. The inner voice knows how each of your encounters are designed specifically for you. The inner voice knows the uniqueness of your journey and, as Harari reveals, "knows that your experiences are a never to be repeated string of experiences." Your inner voice is your director.

You and your experiences elicit light that illuminates the world stage. This light radiates different perspectives on situations.

St. Paul, "everything exposed to the light becomes visible, and everything that is illuminated itself becomes light itself."

Your inner voice, your director, is channeled from the universe. Each living thing on the world stage has their own director. Some hear the director early in life, some later, and some only in their final hours.

Every individual yearns to experience the world, follow their inner voice, and in the right setting, express their inner truths.

Peter Santos, "our freedom lies in remaining open continuously, not only to life's changes but also to the divine light within us and others."

The stage varies for everyone.

Harari, "wherever you choose to be is the right place for you, and you should seek as much freedom as possible to experience the world, listen to your inner voice and express your very own truth."

Individual 'free will' is a human right.

'Free will' trumps state, society, religion, and any other form of control that stifles your inner voice.

Harari, "if the stage is right for the individual's inner voice, then the more liberty individuals have."

Liberty on the world stage allows life to flourish.   Liberty in individuals allows inner peace to radiate from them. They recognize the 'light' of liberty, being at one with the universe.

Sunday Adelaja, "breakthrough is guaranteed if there is enough light."

The stage is set up as a learning environment each day. It is designed specifically for you and the lessons you desire to master in this life.

The location of your 'school room' changes, but every day is an opportunity to master the lesson noted in your script. You, as the co-author of the script, value your dharma.

We go to sleep each night, review our script, and awaken to new lessons on our new stage.

Some lessons you master quickly. Others are more difficult and may take a lifetime or more.

You have at least one teacher to help you master the new lesson. Teachers can be visible and invisible.

A Buddhist proverb, "when the student is ready, the teacher will appear."

Each moment is a 'teachable' opportunity. Each moment allows for the expansion of our awareness.

Being open to your special effects, your signs, your markers assist you in mastering each lesson.

Eckhart Tolle, "life is the dancer, and you are the dance."

Enjoy the universal soundtrack and your dance on your stage.

MARCUS TULLIUS CICERO, "AN ACTOR DOES NOT need to remain on stage throughout a play. It is enough that he appears in the appropriate acts. Likewise, a wise man need not stay on the stage of the world until the audience applauds at the end. The time allotted to our lives may be short, but it is long enough to live honestly and decently. That life is like a play. A good actor knows when to leave the stage."

STAGE SETTINGS

Play

Plato, "you can discover more about a person in an hour of play than in a year of conversation."

Children are unconstrained in their play. Maria Montessori, "play is the work of the child" is a statement most early childhood educators would endorse.

As an educator, mother and nain, it is a pleasure to watch children play.

As I walk by outside play areas, I enjoy hearing children's voices and squeals of laughter, listening to their conversations, and observing their problem-solving skills.

Play is a natural healing therapy. To continue to play throughout your life is a form of holistic medicine.

Deepak Chopra regards play as "an arena for new possibilities and a willingness to escape our routines so we can enjoy life-long creativity." He went on to say, "letting go as done through play can open doors to new discoveries and enables us to feel truly alive. To play is to enjoy opportunities to explore free of outside opinions and artificial boundaries."

Play is one of the few times when we are mask-less. Play is a natural meditative state.

> *We don't stop playing*
> *Because we grow old*
> *We grow old because*
> *We stop playing.*

GEORGE BERNARD SHAW

BEING MASK-LESS CAN ALSO OCCUR DURING meditation, sleep, naps, daydreams, and any 'free time'.

I call these 'nobody' times, mask-less times. I just am.

Deepak Chopra, "our spirits are the true source of creativity."

During play, our spirit is unrestricted and can spontaneously express its inner creative wisdom.

To play is to be in the NOW, and Deepak Chopra feels it "allows our inner reservoir to be slowly released." Playtime is escape time, still time, or as Deepak Chopra calls it, "down-time where joy can appear."

Play is timeless and allows, as Deepak Chopra sees it, your "creative channels to open for all to see."

From a teacher and parent's perspective, you see a different child during their playtime. They are more content, confident, optimistic, and through play, discover new possibilities.

Children discover how the world functions and their space in it via play.

Most playgrounds in developed countries are safe. Parents and guardians permit their children to wander and explore freely.

Jos de Blok, "unstructured play is nature's remedy for boredom."

I recall arriving early one morning to a site in Kolkata. I noticed a group of shoeless young boys playing a game of cricket. There came a point in setting up the location that the boys knew they had to find another area to continue their game.

The boys quietly packed up their things, walked gracefully and knowingly along a high, crumbling stonewall with their simple belongings and bare feet. I was captivated by their effortless movement and silent acknowledgment; it was time to move on. I could hear their laughter, cheering, and enjoyment of their play in the distance.

Now, as a nain, one of my greatest joys is to see my grandchildren play. I cherish having the time to watch their creativity being expressed in so many inventive ways. May each of us, young and old, revisit play often and just be.

CARL JUNG, "THE CREATION OF SOMETHING NEW IS not accomplished by the intellect, but by the PLAY instinct acting from inner necessity. The creative mind plays with the objects it loves."

Home

Pierce Brown, "home isn't where you're from, it's where you find light when all grows dark."

There are times in life when people stay HOME for many reasons. During our recent pandemic, most of the planet was asked to stay home.

And The People Stayed Home

And people stayed home
And read books and listened
And rested and exercised
And made art and played
And learned new ways of being
And stopped
And listened deeper
Someone meditated
Someone prayed
Someone danced

Someone met their shadow
And people began to think differently
And people healed
And in the absence of people
Who lived in ignorant ways,
Dangerous, meaningless, and heartless
Even the earth began to heal
And when the danger ended
And people found each other
Grieved for the dead people,
And they made new choices
And dreamed of new visions
And created new ways of life
And healed the world completely
Just as they were healed themselves.

CATHERINE O'MEARA

WHERE YOU LIVE IS A MIRROR OF YOU AND YOUR vibration.

Charles Dickens, "home is a name, a word, it is a strong one; stronger than magician ever spoke, or spirit ever answered to, in the strongest conjuration."

Sometimes you enter a home and find it uncomfortable. You cannot put a finger on why, but you cannot wait to move on.

In other homes, you feel at ease and can easily settle in for a pleasant visit. Why is this so? Is it to do with the vibration of the house, the people, or the possessions within it?

Leo Tolstoy, "there is no greatness where there is not simplicity, goodness, and truth."

Clutter can affect vibration and trigger homes to feel dense and uncomfortable. Albert Einstein, "everything in life is vibration."

Daniel Silva, "being unburdened by property and possessions."

It is in our nature to be in a minimalistic space, with only the essentials.

In our original home, 'the universe', we had no possessions and wandered the vastness of the universe burdenless. We had no constraints and felt total freedom. We did not even have a physical body. We were totally free.

In the Gospel of Matthew, 19th Chapter, "again, I tell you it is easier for a camel to go through the eye of a needle than for someone who is rich to enter the kingdom of God."

Are we longing for that sense of being unburdened, and are we constantly seeking it?

We are but energy and require open space to flow freely throughout our day.

Panache Desai, "energy like you has no beginning and no end. It can never be destroyed. It is only ever shifting states."

Homes that are cluttered hinder energy flow. Fewer possessions allow your energy to shift freely.

We came into this dimension with no material possessions and leave with no material attachments.

Buddha, "life is suffering, attachment is the source of suffering. The end of attachment will bring the end of suffering."

We have been programmed since an early age to be consumers. Brand labels have been the cause of much anxiety for many individuals.

The Dalai Lama, "most of our troubles are due to our passionate desire for and attachment to things that we misapprehend as enduring entities."

I wear an inexpensive watch for teaching and travel. I usually purchase one with a ribbon band. My most recent watch has a red/blue watch band. When I teach, I am always amazed at the number of children who ask me if my watch is a Gucci.

I always leave my watch in a developing country. I like the circle the watch has traveled.

Happiness is not found
In things you possess.
But in what you have
The courage to release.

Nathaniel Hawthorne

I love the story of Gandhi and his sandal. Gandhi, when boarding a train, lost a sandal. Gandhi quickly threw the remaining sandal out onto the tracks. When questioned why, he replied, "I threw the other sandal because whoever finds the first sandal, wouldn't it be nice if they found the other one as well?"

When traveling in developing countries, you see a less materialistic world. In their rural areas, there are mainly austere dwellings. You frequently observe mothers cleaning with homemade brooms.

They have rituals and routines for tending their homes. Their housework is simple, as they have few possessions. Families spend time outside with nature. They use their dwelling mainly for sleeping.

Life is simple and uncomplicated. There is a thin veil between their day and night. During their sleep, they return to even more space.

Epicurus, it is "not what we have but what we enjoy, constitute our abundance."

About ten years ago, I was a volunteer on a team in Uganda. We had just finished helping children and visited the Nile River rapids on our way back to our accommodations. We departed our van and began to walk toward the Nile rapids.

As we strolled, we passed many simple homes. You could see women sweeping and hear children laughing. As we approached the rapids, one homestead caught my attention. It was an immaculate small piece of property. It had a well-maintained bamboo fence, a flourishing vegetable garden, and a fruit tree. A man waved to us.

We arrived at the Nile rapids; what a beautiful place. Rushing, bubbling water flowing over large boulders and smaller debris. We each found our own spot. Some sat, some stood, some wandered.

The man, who had waved to us from his home, strode by. He had a handsome toothless smile, faded orange-tattered clothing, bare feet, and a 'magical' way about him. He was carrying a simple, well-used, homemade bamboo fishing rod.

He headed to the Nile rapids with confidence. I watched him leapfrog from rock to rock and choose his spot to fish. I remember thinking to myself at the time; this is the happiest man I have ever seen. It was one of those 'awe' moments.

To be a minimalist is the beginning of being free from the material world. Your home often reflects you.

If your home is cluttered and disorganized, then you tend to have a cluttered, busy mind.

Consumption is never-ending.

'Less is more' is achievable with a strong will and practice.

If your home is spacious regardless of the area, then the occupant(s) tend to be more open and flexible.

When in Uganda, as a volunteer, I recall another special scene.

We had just completed helping children. One of the little boys was not feeling well. I am guessing he was about eight years old. Most of our deserving children suffer from malnutrition and/or malaria; as a result, it is difficult to tell the child's age.

I asked a Ugandan friend to help me walk the young boy to his caregiver. In Uganda, there are 52 dialects. My friend spoke the dialect of this area of Uganda.

We were told by other children where the boy's caregiver was. I remember it was a particularly hot day. We walked across a field with no vegetation, just bare, scorched ground.

In Uganda, many caregivers are grandparents, as countless parents died due to the AIDS pandemic.

As we approached the little boy's caregiver, we saw an elderly man standing beside his old, worn bicycle. He was surrounded by young children. We learned this was our little boy's grandfather, his caregiver.

The other children with him were all his grandchildren. He was the sole caregiver for all these young children. We helped him strap the boy's new supplies onto his well-used bike.

They were all so happy to now have these new useful items. We asked the grandfather how they would use the one ground sheet. He said they would all put their heads on the ground sheet, using it as a pillow for each child.

The grandfather said to his young grandson, who had just received his supplies, that he now owned more than he had in his life.

Uganda was a, never to be repeated, schoolroom for each of us.

Deepak Chopra, "with thought and effort you can create an environment that supports your success and enables you to feel positive and alive. Enjoy your home and workspace by making simple changes that will allow your environment to enhance your life."

Your soul is in the temple of your body. Your body is mostly in the temple of your home. In the sanctity of your home, your deepest thoughts often occur. It is where your day begins and where you lay your head at the end of the day.

Deepak Chopra, "my outer world reflects my inner world."

Sleep and Dreams

WILLIAM SHAKESPEARE, "O SLEEP, O GENTLE SLEEP. Nature's soft nurse."

If I am away, I start reorganizing as soon as I am shown my room. It always starts with the bed. When in developing countries, there is less to do as the rooms are often basic, which speaks to me.

I always travel with a box of Bounce to developing countries. I have been told it deters cockroaches, mosquitoes, etc. I am not certain it does, but it makes me feel more comfortable, if only for the scent.

I always travel with a pillowcase, and my own cotton sleeping bag, just in case. Once I set up the bed, I clear away all unnecessary bits and pieces, check out the washroom situation, check my window and view (if there is one) and prepare for my sleep.

At home in Canada, sheets, duvet, and pillows are always fresh. Ventilation is important to me. I always have the window open, even with harsh Canadian winters. I prefer no rugs and curtains. I always like to glimpse nature.

I recall my mother, who was in her 90s and in the last scene of her life, saying to me, "see that tree," and pointed to her window. I said, "yes, mom." Then with passion in her voice, she said, "that's my friend."

My last connection to the day I have just lived is to internally thank 10 'things' that touched me during my day.

Maya Angelo, "let gratitude be the pillow upon which you kneel to say your nightly prayer."

I have complete trust and honor for the healing power of my body. I surrender into my prayer, "body heal thyself," as I close my day.

Bernie Siegel, "the body gets the message that he loves his life, and the body does all it can to help him survive and thrive."

On our life journey, we sleep the most at the beginning of our life and at the end of our life. Newborns require sleep to grow physically and mentally. In your final scene, 'letting go' often occurs through your peaceful sleep.

It is sleep to which we return each night to review and edit our script for the following day. After a good night's sleep, one is prepared and provided with the tools to have a successful and purposeful new day.

Michael Singer, "life is molding me each day to become who I needed to be in order to handle tomorrow's tasks."

When I awake each morning, I try to think of my day as a large blank artist's canvas.

Michael Singer, "with the skill of Picasso painting a masterpiece on the blank canvas of people's minds."

I begin painting my canvas with the agenda I would like to accomplish during my day. I am fresh from sleep, having reviewed my script and potential lessons that may be acquired in my new, stimulating day.

I use vivid colors and the colors of the rainbow to create my brand-new day.

If events in my day slowly turn negative, I remove the dark colors that have seeped in and replace them with bright, cheerful colors. I have internalized Michael Singer's words, "when dark clouds become rainbows."

These words remind me of Nelson Mandela and his incarceration at Robben Island. Nelson Mandela was a South African anti-apartheid activist. He received more than 250 honors, including the Nobel Peace Prize.

Nelson Mandela had a predominantly positive mindset. He was a visionary and could see the big picture, the world stage.

The ability to turn a negative into a positive or seeing your glass as half-full rather than half-empty is a technique to elicit sunshine and brightness in your day.

Sleep revitalizes our body and reconnects each of us to our script and our inner wisdom. The body communicates to us through our dreams.

Eleanor Roosevelt, "the future belongs to those who believe in the beauty of their dreams."

Sleep is a natural meditative state. The body cannot talk, but it can communicate to us through our dreams.

Sleep allows the mind to be quiet, like a still pond. Possibly our inner truths are mirrored in the reflection of the calm pool.

Sleep is the ultimate silence and your escape from a busy day. Sleep is a 'letting go' experience and perhaps preparation for your last scene.

Do we die each night? Do we leave the old me in our sleep and greet the new me after sleep? Is sleep a porthole connecting dimensions?

Michio Kaku, "I sometimes wonder whether such patients who have temporal lobe epilepsy have access to another dimension of reality, a wormlike of sorts, into another dimension."

Perhaps sleep connects each of us to our script and our higher wisdom.

Michael Singer, "our higher self is able to whisper to our lower self through sleep. Sleep is our higher self-realm, where all is possible, infinite possibilities. Sleep allows our higher forces to engage with each other. Often hope appears after a good night sleep."

Possibly during sleep, you allow your higher self to take the helm of your vessel.

You recognize that you are in safe hands and feel positive that with time and patience, you will return to a safe harbor. Are you surrendering to the universal script?

During sleep, meditation, prayer, or a resting state, you organize your tools, your teachers for the next lesson to be studied.

Michael Singer, "at some point there's no more struggle, just the deep peace that comes from surrendering to a perfection that is beyond your comprehension."

I recall retiring from teaching after 32 years. I was fifty-five, mentally and physically sound. I knew there was more to do. Time for new dreams!

I had always lived a purposeful life. Why stop now?

I started traveling to developing countries as a helper and shifted into substitute teaching. These were new scene and mask changes for me! I had new dreams to materialize into my reality.

When I reflect on my journey, I am so connected to my life script. Being a teacher and all the gifts that come with this noble profession had activated the skills that entered with me from the universe.

Michael Singer, allowing "life to become your friend, your teacher, and your secret lover."

My passion and belief in children and their gifts have propelled me forward all my life.

I have come to appreciate that children worldwide are the treasured gifts of the universe.

A mother's love for each child is the same everywhere. A father's need to protect and provide is the same everywhere.

Parents everywhere dream of a better life for their children. It is a universal dream.

I internalize Michael Singer's words, "when life's way becomes your way, all the noise stops and there is a great peace."

My connection to my script is strengthened through my 'still time' and nature. I try to live in the NOW.

I practice Hermes Trismegistus's words, "as within, so without."

I prepare for sleep and 'to receive' my tools and teachers for my new day, for my new me.

I often internally ask for help with parts of my life or myself that I am struggling with.

Being aware of your dreams helps to create the new reality of your new day. The words and pictures from your dreams are like a 'muddled up' movie due to 'free will'.

Michio Kaku, "the areas of the brain that are activated during sleep are the same as those involved in learning a new task."

'Free will' is our silent guide to the choices in our day. All of this is 'blessed' with pure love. All done with the intention that you complete and be successful with the lesson you are toiling on.

Often the lesson is not learned the first time, and that is OK. It is in your agreement, your script, to take as long as necessary to complete your lesson. Our spiritual journey is an infinite one.

I OFTEN THINK OF MARTIN LUTHER KING JR'S words as I close my eyes, "I have a dream…"

Caste

Isabel Wilkerson, "caste is the wordless usher in a dark theatre, flashlight cast down in the aisle, guiding us to our assigned seats for a performance."

Many souls have chosen the lower caste to enact their role, purpose, and lessons to be taught and mastered on their journey.

It is interesting to note that the difference in spelling between a cast of actors and caste in the social hierarchy pyramid is an 'e'.

While helping in Kolkata, we visited a poor area on the city's outskirts. Many of the inhabitants were refugees from Bangladesh. Their accommodations were minimal, overcrowded, and on land that continually flooded.

A young girl washing dishes in the open field caught my eye. I am guessing she was about eight years old. She had thick, black, shiny hair and large white teeth. She was squatting in front of a large tin pail filled with water and to one side was an enormous pile of dirty pots and pans.

I had so many emotions rushing through me. But her gaze comforted me. She was doing her job. In her way, she was content.

I thought of all the eight-year-old children I had taught. They would be here if this had been their chosen role in their script. Maybe in their next life, they will be, or perhaps they have been this little girl. Maybe I have been a child like her?

On a visit to the Gandhi Museum in Madurai, I met a scholarly, middle-aged man who had studied Gandhi's life. I walked with him through the museum. Towards the end of the exhibit, there was a glass encasement with Gandhi's bloodied dhoti. He had been wearing the dhoti the day he had been assassinated.

The man explained that days before Gandhi had been shot, he had said to one of his disciples that this reincarnation was coming to an end. His wish was that he would reincarnate as an 'untouchable' in his next life.

Gandhi had dedicated his life to defending the 'untouchables' but did not know what it was like to live as an untouchable. His wish, in his next life, was to reincarnate as a Dalit and to live their 'truths'.

The caste pyramid is in all societies. When I am exposed to lower caste souls, I am content in their presence.

I recall frequently visiting a slum area in Cuba with my mom. She verbalized to me numerous times, "this is where I am my happiest, visiting with these souls."

Interestingly, in the Cuban caste system, many doctors, lawyers, and teachers live in the poorer areas. The higher

Cuban caste hierarchy is found in the service industry. Tourists can be very generous.

Through my journey, I grew to understand and value my mother's words.

As an educator, I was aware of a hierarchy system. I spent several years teaching in a low socio-economic school. At least once a week, there was a police car parked in the school's driveway. The police were often assisting with a 'situation'.

Many of the parents of my students were young, single moms. Many lived in subsidized housing; many lived off mother's allowance.

However, their love and dedication to their children was endless. They aspired for more for their children. They were supportive of me as their child's teacher. We were a team striving to provide the best for their child.

After I left that school, I kept in touch with many of the parents. Several of their children completed college and more. Their successes were anchored in the love and support from their parents.

My life has been enriched by my time amid lower caste children. I am a better person. I know their day, their dreams, their hopes, and I 'bless' each of them.

I hope in some small way I helped to facilitate their 'wings to fly'.

FRIEDRICH NIETZSCHE, "HE WHO HAS A WHY TO LIVE can bear almost any how."

Actors

Johann Wolfgang von Goethe perceived life as a quarry "out of which we are to mold and chisel and complete a character."

Our character is slowly revealed from the universal clay. It is sculpted by universal hands into a fine museum-quality artifact.

All your experiences, both positive and negative, have been penned into your script for your growth.

We are constantly evolving.

The 'you' of yesterday is molded slightly differently than the 'you' of today.

Akemi, "we are like actors who come onto the stage, and we are only taking on various roles in the play for the time being."

The word 'person' comes from the Latin word persona, a mask formerly worn by Greek actors.

Joseph Murphy, "in ancient times, the Greek actor put on a mask and assumed the role of the person depicted by the mask. He dramatized, through the mask, the characteristics and qualities of the personality it suggested."

During each scene, our mask can transform according to our script and the lessons we are here to learn.

Joseph Murphy, "simply changing your self-image from weak and disempowerment to strong and powerful is only changing your mask."

Each mask and scene serve its role on the world stage. It is a coordinated effort and precisely timed for a successful performance.

Joseph Murphy, "when you change your mask, you change your thought pattern."

We each have access to our higher self, where your script originated.

When we consider and do actions for others, when we notice nature and all its bounties, when we are peaceful, joyful, and balanced within, when we are 'open' to the universal wisdom, when we have a healthy ego, then we are there with our higher self, our soul.

By uttering 'yes' to life, "you are saying yes to all the ideas which heal, bless, inspire, elevate, and strengthen your life," wrote Joseph Murphy.

Stating 'yes' to life is saying yes to your script.

A new mask and scene change occurs when a new role is about to begin in your script.

Joseph Murphy, "you are here to lead a happy, full and glorious life. You are here to release your hidden talents to the world, and to find your true place in life."

Each actor is a star.

Each actor is unique.

Each actor is essential to the success of the performance on the world stage.

Each actor is special for the gifts that accompanied them from the universe.

No two actors are alike.

Joseph Murphy, "an infinite differentiation is the law of life, and there is no such thing as an unneeded person."

Everything and everyone is an eminent part of the play.

No actor is superior. We are all equals.

Your role on the world stage is vital to its success.

Joseph Murphy, "your subconscious is your most powerful friend. Your subconscious watches over you while you sleep and controls all your vital processes."

Your subconscious is your director. Your director facilitated the writing of your script. Your subconscious is your higher self, your soul.

Your subconscious knows ALL. It knows your past, present, and future journeys. It values your infinite script.

Your director is non-critical and is at one with the universe's wisdom.

Joseph Murphy, "the interaction of your conscious and subconscious mind is the basis of all the events of your life."

Your conscious is your lower self. Your subconscious is your higher self. Your journey is the union of your lower self and your higher self.

Albert Einstein, "I know that philosophically a murderer is not responsible for his crime," but he went on to say, "I prefer not to take tea with him."

As mentioned by Einstein, this actor, this murderer, this lower self is following his script and his 'free will'.

Choices were made by this actor.

I reflect on Einstein's words when listening to the world news.

We each follow our script. We do not know the journey other souls have experienced thus far in their life. Should this lead, after the consequences of their actions, to non-judgment and forgiveness?

Roman Krznaric wrote we are "merely bit players, appearing on stage for the briefest moment in a story stretching over eons."

Perhaps in our infinite universal script we each role-play various characters, including heroes and villains.

In the early years of your life, you are constantly experimenting with your masks. A mask feels right for a certain scene.

Eventually, there is a need to explore and appraise a different mask for another scene change.

Entrances and exits on the world stage are frequent, like a revolving door.

Jen Sincero, "the universe wants you to grow and bloom into the most glorious version of yourself."

During our early years, we are seeking to decipher the 'game of life'.

Once a source of passion is realized, 'teachers' emerge to guide the development of the passion.

Angela Duckworth, "purpose is a tremendously powerful source of motivation."

The passion mask slowly transitions on. This passage takes time.

The journey for a new mask fitting requires patience and understanding of this delicate and timely adjustment.

A pregnant woman's sensitive journey from conception to birth is transitional. The changes in the mother's physical body, the sharing of her body with her child. The parents making healthy choices so that the mother and child can thrive.

Elizabeth Hay, "you knew a change was coming, you even knew what form it would take, but the details varied, the struggle varied, the language varied."

Some transitional souls seek guidance with this change. There are many resources available for this shift in the mental health community.

You are not alone. Your teachers, angels, and support actors are all cheering for you.

Others just trust, as Elizabeth Hay writes, "I lied down in the stream of life and let it, flow over me."

Transitions occur at the precise right moment in the universal script.

Angela Duckworth, "changes are preprogrammed."

Each entrance and exit flow with the dance of life.

Angela Duckworth, "we change when we need to."

The mask transition can occur with a new job, at your wedding, your child's birth, taking care of an aging or sickly family member, a passing, or graduation. Wherever and whenever there is change, there is a potential for a mask and scene transition.

New feelings may arise while the new mask is being molded, and preparations for the new lesson to be learned are transitioned in.

It takes time for these new feelings and emotions to feel comfortable with the new scene and mask.

Elizabeth Hay, "one day something relaxed inside, and I saw things in a new way."

Each passage has a unique feel to it.

One aspiration is to raise our vibration during this life journey.

This goal is accomplished by an 'openness' to all of life's elements and pleasant surprises.

Elizabeth Hay, "he felt life ripple thru, connecting him to every other living thing and his own existence was the least of it and the most of it."

Each evolution phase is different.

Transitions may feel, as Elizabeth Hay alludes to, "like wings folding about him."

Each manifestation of a new mask and new scene is a sacred moment in universal time. As the newly sculpted mask emerges and a new scene materializes, the script and journey continue.

We mature as we proceed on our life journey following our script.

Angela Duckworth, "we adapt in response to the growing demands of our circumstances."

Our lives become full; we parse out quiet times whenever and wherever possible.

Days, months, years float by, and baby steps move each of us forward.

Mask and scenes slowly recede as they fulfill their purpose.

Angela Duckworth, "new ways of thinking and acting become durable and finally become our identity."

Mask and scene changes become seamless.

You have adapted to the dance, the flow of your script.

William James, "the old in the new is what claims the attention. The old with a slightly new turn."

The mid-years are for deciding on the masks needed to fulfill our dharma.

We experiment with our masks until we are at one with our passion.

We are remembering and, in Angela Duckworth's words, "practicing lines in our script."

The time varies with each souls script, but our purpose to help others emerges.

Angela Duckworth, "the intention to contribute to the well-being of others" is inherent in each of us and hovers throughout each of our journeys.

We are ALL in this together, on the world stage.

We recognize the cast of characters in our lives. Our support actors who have made our journey flow from one line to the next in our script.

We become mindful of other souls scripts.

Angela Duckworth, "people first become attracted to things they enjoy and later appreciate how these personal interests might also benefit others. We start out with a self-oriented interest, then learn self-discipline practice and finally integrate that work with another purpose to help others other than ourselves."

We are slowly transitioning from a singular life to a global life according to the timing of each script.

I personally felt this passage as I retired from teaching. My teaching mask receded. A traveling helper mask materialized.

My teaching years supported my new mask.

I internally knew I was following the 'flow' of my script. I was flowing into a global citizen.

As you move toward the final mask and scene changes, some days feel like you are pressing your foot on the accelerator of your life.

Our many mask and scene changes have served us well.

But time is moving on, and a review of our script reminds us there are more 'things' to accomplish.

David Brook, "we have spent long days and evenings of toil."

We have weathered in Angela Duckworth's words, "setbacks and disappointments and struggles. All of this is worth it because ultimately the efforts will pay dividends to other people."

In these final scenes, you begin to put your life, thus far, under your own inner personal magnifying glass.

Each scene, each mask change is analyzed. You begin to see your script. You begin to see the answers to your own personal questions, such as, "why am I here?"

You start to observe the reasons for your exits and entrances, your purpose of this reincarnation, this life.

You begin to see all the positive and 'light', of your life.

You acknowledge the dark and negative times as well.

David Brook, "and then there are moments maybe toward middle or old age, when the leopard comes down from the hills and just sits there in the middle of your door frame. He stares at you inescapably. He demands your justification. There are no excuses at that moment. Everybody has to throw off their mask."

Our final scenes are often when the 'awe' moment is more frequent.

Rabbi Heschel describes awe as "an act of insight into a meaning greater than ourselves."

We have realized our purpose and now want to help others.

We aspire for less; our wants and desires have been realized.

We wear fewer masks. The call from the universe is now a whisper. We are beginning our journey home.

Armando Lucas Correa, "lightness is essential from the moment you decide to leave."

We are reviewing our script and accepting, if not in this life, maybe in the next.

Roman Krznaric, "we are just a passing moment in a far bigger, longer narrative."

As we transition into the final scenes, we prepare to pass on our dance card to the next dancer.

We begin to prepare for the final curtain call.

There is now a 'knowing feeling' as you slowly transition toward your 'universal mask.'

THICH NHAT HANH, "WE ARE HERE TO AWAKEN from our illusion of separateness."

SUPPORT FOR ACTORS

Entrances and Exits

Bernie Siegal, "actors going on stage in a well-rehearsed role."

We know our script. We know our lines, and we know the masks we will wear.

This knowledge is within each of us and will surface at the exact right time by our director, our higher self.

Our entrance on the world stage is with our birth, our first mask, and scene.

Albert Einstein, "you and I never cease to stand like curious children before the great mystery into which we were born."

Your mask, as a newborn, involves your dependency, on your caregivers, for all your essential needs.

Deepak Chopra, "newborns come from the realm of pure awareness."

As a newborn, you are observing and just taking it all in. Your every need is met with love and adoration.

You grow rapidly and become less reliant on your caregivers.

Anthony Doerr felt that caregivers set 'the stage' for the child.

Caregivers are instrumental in nurturing and preparing their children to share the gifts they brought from the universe.

Children are observing, processing, and modeling the actions they witness.

James Baldwin, "children have never been good at listening to their elders, but they have never failed to imitate them."

I experienced these words as a mother and a teacher. I was a primary teacher for many years.

One of my greatest 'joys' was to see a child transition from a non-reader to a reader. This transition can happen quickly, or it can take time.

Reading is a mask and scene change for a learner.

The skill of reading is an awareness expansion for each student.

Books were a focus in my own family. My eldest son adored the book 'The Little Engine That Could'.

My aunt, who was also an educator, gave the book to our toddler.

Night after night, we read that book. One night I was reading/modeling, paused, and my son continued reading. He knew when to turn the page and completed reading the book to me.

Before my eyes, I saw his mask and scene change. His love of books became a permanent mask.

As other teachers arrive in the child's life, mask changes become more frequent. Each teacher guides the child.

Angela Duckworth, "master teachers create an environment."

As a young student, you are fresh from the universe. You are keen and open to learning your lessons.

Angela Duckworth, "I glimpsed the possibility that a child's connection with a teacher can be life-changing from birth."

Your seeds of passion for your script came with you from the universe.

They are planted in your subconscious. Each teacher the student encounters will begin to nourish the seeds.

Each teacher will share their 'magic' with each student.

In Angela Duckworth's words, the student will slowly learn "to stop, breathe and fully connect with their lived experience."

Pablo Casals, "the child must know that he/she is a miracle, that since the beginning of the world there hasn't been and until the end of the world there will not be, another child like him/her."

Angela Duckworth, each child "has a calling."

Each child waits patiently for their call.

When hearing their call, the child will make the world a better place.

Educators acknowledge each child's gifts and nurture them.

Educators form a team with the student and their parents to facilitate the support and environment for each student's gifts.

Children ask questions, which arouse their internal gifts.

Naturalist, "hands-on experiences at the critical time, not systematic knowledge, is what counts in the making of a naturalist. Better to spend long stretches of time just searching and dreaming."

Each child has had a 'dress rehearsal' in the universe before their birth.

They practiced the lines in their script, knew when mask and scene changes would occur. They knew they had a loving internal director who was always there, gently guiding their evolution. They knew their many entrances and exits on the world stage, their time-outs, their reflective times.

E. O. Wilson, "a child comes to the edge of deep water with a mind prepared for wonder."

Student's thought patterns and imagination are materialized into their school room scene at the appropriate time.

Anthony Doerr, "a child is born, the world sets in upon it. Taking things away and stuffing things into it."

The child's mask slowly transitions when their innocence fades. A new mask is molded with the passage to the material world.

Through trial and error involving many mask and scene changes, many entrances and exits, each actor will eventually discover a vocation that will enhance their gifts.

Angela Duckworth, "a job that will be meaningful to society."

A vocation that will nourish their soul and provide them with a purposeful life.

E.E. Cummings, "it takes courage to grow up and become who you really are."

Body

William Shakespeare, "our bodies are our gardens to which our wills are gardener."

Just as an actor has costumes for their performance, so do souls have a particular body type for this life.

Buddha, "our body is precious. It is our vehicle for awakening. Treat it with care."

Keeping our body at its peak performance is our commitment to ourselves and our script.

Our body is our temple.

Deepak Chopra, "to keep the body in good health is a duty – otherwise, we shall not be able to keep our mind strong and clear."

Our bodies are always seeking balance.

It is our body, through gradual change, which supports us through our life cycle.

Deepak Chopra, "our evolutionary impulse to progress in our lives is to seek and attain balance and to be healthy and strong."

Each body type has its own challenges, according to each script.

Each body type is chosen for a learning style that is unique to you and will provide comfort and trials.

I believe the more difficult the life experience, the higher the vibration attained. The late Stephen Hawking is an excellent example of this.

Stephen Hawking was a Cambridge University physicist and best-selling author. He was diagnosed with ALS at 21. He slowly lost control of his muscles. He was confined to a wheel-chair and spoke through a speech synthesizer. He became a symbol of determination and curiosity.

While helping in the Philippines, I observed numerous children with cleft palates and other challenges. I internally 'blessed' each of their journeys on the world stage.

An intention of the Universal Script is to raise your vibration during your lifetime. Your body welcomes the many vibrational transitions.

The raised vibration allows you to see through universal eyes and to see your connection to ALL.

Watching a child during their day is to see the body at its peak.

A child's day flows from one adventure to the next.

Play is their work time, physical activity is constant, eating is a pause only when needed, sleep and downtime are their 'still time'.

Hippocrates, "the natural healing force within each of us is the greatest force in getting well."

'Body heal thyself' is trusting your body to do what is necessary to return you to the game of life and to be at one with your script.

RALPH WALDO EMERSON, "MOST OF THE SHADOWS of this life are caused by standing in one's own sunshine."

Movement

Aldous Huxley, "consciousness is only possible through change, change is only possible through movement."

In the beginning, we were all hunters and gatherers.

As hunters and gatherers, we used all our physical and mental energy to search for food and water for our families.

By becoming sedentary, we have turned the positive energy of hunting and gathering into negative energy.

Deepak Chopra views yoga as a "union of body, mind, and spirit."

I began my yoga practice years ago with simple positions. With time and listening to my body, my daily practice slowly grew.

I feel fit and flexible because of my yoga practice.

My mind is quieter and receptive to new experiences and adventures.

Activity facilitates the release of stress and negativity.

When you exercise, your body releases chemicals in your brain. These 'feel good' compounds enhance being positive. They assist in eliminating one's feelings of being overwhelmed and anxious.

Have you ever noticed when moments of agitation visit you, your immediate response is to move?

Movement provides your brain with a workout. Exercise can improve memory and increase energy levels.

Without exercise, negativity keeps recycling through your consciousness.

Sensations from movement can provide a compelling counter-argument to these adverse thought patterns.

Movement facilitates new thoughts and can lead you to move in a positive 'new way'.

Movement creates space and allows you to abandon old thoughts and actions.

Movement is in our natural world. Everything moves.

When you become part of the movement, you connect to the vibration of the universe.

Deepak Chopra, "movement is like a dance" and through your action, you become a partner in the universal dance.

Movement occurs in all manners. It allows the 'new you' of the day to come forth.

As you move, all your senses are activated; you become open to receiving the 'magic' of your unique day.

Movement is one of my modes of meditation. A walk or a bike ride with nature allows me to feel the vibration of my surroundings.

I know, instinctively, that I prepare for my life lessons here. I feel connected to my higher self and its infinite wisdom.

For me, fresh thoughts and ideas come with this connection facilitated by movement.

Exercise allows you to be selective as to the stimuli you internalize.

Movement activates a 'screening mechanism', and once resting after being active, that which needs to be accomplished becomes apparent.

Movement is like refocusing a 'blurry screen'. The picture of your day becomes clearer.

Life is movement and change.

Change is the release of old patterns that have predominately served you well. Change allows the 'new you', to transition in.

I was twenty-three when I became a teacher.

I would leave school soon after the bell rang and go for a long run.

My lesson plan for the next day would transition in during my run. Thoughts of my students would flash before me, and I would be alerted to some issues that needed my attention.

The following day, I would wake up early, arrive at school, and eagerly set up my classroom for the new day.

Action shifts our awareness and helps us to recognize the space we are in and how to use it wisely.

Movement rebalances our perspectives, improves our physiology, and allows us to experience all aspects of ourselves.

Through activity, we feel flexible, empowered, and in balance.

Movement can shift our mood, our self-image.

Movement is a valuable tool in our supportive toolkit.

> *Life is like a bicycle.*
> *To keep your balance,*
> *You must keep moving.*

ALBERT EINSTEIN

Gratitude

Happiness cannot be
traveled to,
owned
worn
or consumed.
Happiness
is the spiritual experience
of living every minute
with
LOVE,
GRACE,
and
GRATITUDE.

DENIS WAITLEY

AS THE CURTAIN LOWERS ON YOUR DAY, BEING grateful and recognizing all the bounties which you received is a nice way to depart your day.

Rumi, "wear gratitude like a cloak, and it will feed every corner of your life."

I walk or ride my bike, mostly in nature. A certain tree, a peony, a sunset can take my breath away. I internally say 'thank you'.

I acknowledge the scene and feel it has been choreographed specifically for me at this precise moment. I feel 'awe' and linger.

Deepak Chopra, "gratitude shifts our awareness, changing our approach to others and the world."

Gratitude offers a 'weightless' feeling as you connect to the NOW.

> *Gratitude is an essential part of being present.*
> *When you go deeply into the present.*
> *Gratitude arises spontaneously.*
>
> ECKHART TOLLE

DEEPAK CHOPRA, "GRATITUDE AND THANK YOU HELP us to clear away the noise of our ego and allows us to connect more deeply with our inner wisdom."

Each thank you at the end of the day guides me to a positive new day.

A 'thank you' connects you to a higher vibration.

Meister Eckhart, "if the only prayer you said was thank you, that would be enough."

Being thankful for our day and the lessons presented, sends a positive light to your new day.

Deepak Chopra, "recognizing that we are thankful for what we have in our lives is an important part of our journey to perfect health."

At the end of my day, I thank my family, friends, and community for their support and encouragement. I would not be where I am without them. All angels, visible and invisible, are also thanked.

Deepak Chopra, "sharing what we have learned and thanking those experiences which have helped us to build a supportive community is essential to building a positive lifestyle."

HAVE YOU EARNED YOUR TOMORROW?

Is anybody happier because you passed his way?
Does anyone remember that you spoke to him
*   today?*
This day is almost over, and its toiling time is
*   through,*
Is there anyone to utter now a kindly word
*   of you?*

Did you give a cheerful greeting to the friend
*   who came along?*
Or a churlish sort of "Howdy" and then vanish
*   in the throng?*
Were you selfish pure and simple as you rushed
*   along the way,*
Or is someone mighty grateful for a deed you
*   did today?*

Can you say tonight, in parting with the day
    that's slipping fast,
That you helped a single brother of the many
    that you passed?
Is a heart rejoicing over what you did or said?
Does a man whose hopes were fading, now with
    courage look ahead?

Did you waste the day, or lose it, was it well or
    sorely spent?
Did you leave a trail of kindness or a scar of
    discontent?
As you close your eyes in slumber do you think
    that God would say,
You have earned one more tomorrow by the
    work you did today?

EDGAR GUEST

JOHN MILTON, "GRATITUDE BESTOWS REVERENCE----
changing forever how we experience life and the world."

Smiles

Bill Bryson, "the most universal expression of all is a smile, which is a nice thought."

Smiles are electric. They can change you in a most positive way.

Denis Waitley, "a smile is the light in your window that tells others that there is a caring person inside."

I remember a site in Uganda. Some of the children who had received their supplies and their families were lingering. There was music and dancing.

I noticed a young man dragging himself along the ground towards us.

He had the most beautiful smile. He was about 18 years old. He had polio as a child. Polio had left his legs lifeless.

But still the smile, the unselfish joy for the children who had received their supplies.

The crowd began to disperse. This young man lingered.

I spoke with my Ugandan friend. She agreed to effectuate an apparatus for this young man to move around more readily.

No more dragging himself, a nicer way of moving for this worthy young man. A nicer day!

His huge smile had first spoken to me, not his paralyzed legs.

On a subsequent visit to India, we visited a polio orphanage.

The children's smiles were infectious. They had each received supplies and were overjoyed for us to join them in their daily activities and lunch.

A smile can 'light up your day'. Even on a local walk, I always smile.

Sometimes it comes back.

I know the 'electricity' of a smile and want to share this with everyone and everything I encounter in my day.

JOSEPH ADDISON, "WHAT SUNSHINE IS TO FLOWERS, smiles are to humanity."

Words

Mother Teresa, "kind words can be short and easy to speak, but their echoes are truly endless."

"Hi, please, thank you, and namaste" are kind words.

They create a positive beginning and ending to a scene. Each of these words connects you and the receiver in a receptive space.

Jamie Dimon, "it's what you say and how you say it. How often you say it."

I often say, "good job, good try." I try to keep it positive, short, and upbeat.

Sometimes when entering a potential tense scene, I have an inner conversation and ask for 'help' for the right words.

I am seldom let down. I often find myself part of the audience and am in 'awe' of the words I have been a channel for.

Raise your words, not your voice.
It is rain that grows flowers, not thunder.

RUMI

IN OTHER SITUATIONS, I HAVE HAD PEOPLE SAY TO me your words really helped me.

I know it was not me, but my higher self.

I was just the conduit emitting the right words at the right time.

JOHN KEATING, "NO MATTER WHAT ANYBODY TELLS you, words and ideas can change the world."

Visualization

Michael Singer, "bring the invisible into the visible."

This is the essence of visualizing: to form a mental image and then, with time and patience, transition it to the visible.

As a traveling helper, our team visited several of south India's rural villages.

We helped Dalit children. If lucky to have jobs, their parents worked on farms or had menial jobs.

I met two successful men, both of whom were born in a local village. As young boys, they had both been sent to school in the UK. Life had been good to them.

I recall standing in a field. It was hot, cow dung was everywhere, and lots of flies.

As we swatted away the menacing bugs, they told me about their dreams for this area. They both wanted to 'give back' and to help the region of their birth.

They pointed to where they saw a community center, then in another direction to a school, and in the last direction to where they saw a hospital. A community center, school, and hospital all for the village people.

I witnessed their vision materialize.

Adult 'untouchables' are trained and work in the community center. Dalit children attend the school, where they also receive their meals. Locals use the hospital as needs arise.

Through their commitment to their boyhood home, these two men had manifested the world they aspired for the villagers.

They helped many of the locals, in Deepak Chopra's words, "to recognize their unique talents and abilities."

And to recognize that they too are major actors on the world stage.

When you visualize,
then you materialize.

DENIS WAITLEY

Imagination

Einstein, "THE TRUE SIGN OF INTELLIGENCE IS NOT knowledge, but imagination."

I frequently witnessed Einstein's words in the kindergarten classroom:

I saw potential engineers, architects, and construction workers at building centers.

I saw potential medical personnel at the doll center, bandaging, casting, and using toy medical equipment.

I saw potential artists at the paint, arts, and craft table turning 'junk' into beautiful things.

I saw potential service workers and chefs at the house center, preparing meals, setting, clearing tables, stocking the shelves, and taking inventory.

I saw teachers at the reading center absorbed in books and making worksheets.

I saw scientists at the live science table with microscopes and magnifying glasses examining all our treasures found on nature walks.

I saw accountants and bankers with whiteboards and markers.

I saw entertainers at the puppet and dress-up centers.

I saw gardeners at the growing center pruning, watering, measuring, and talking to our plants.

I saw lawyers making our safety rules and the police enforcing them.

Most years we hatched chick or duck eggs.

We had an incubator. We built ramps and homes for our guests. We had a wading pool for our ducks. Many went for 'sleepovers' with the students.

It was all from each child's imagination.

I love hearing the journeys and 'callings' of my former students.

Logic will get you from A to B,
Imagination will take you everywhere.

ALBERT EINSTEIN

Director

Akemi, "we are not just actors, but also the creative director."

In our temple, we have two selves:

> the actor, your lower self,
>
> the director, your higher self, your soul.

Your director's destiny is wholeness of the self through union of the two: your lower self and your higher self.

Michael Singer, "most of life will unfold in accordance with forces far outside your control."

The Universal Script, better known as the Book of Life and the Akashic Records, has a record of each soul's thoughts, deeds, words, feelings, actions, and intents from the beginning of time, similar to 'cloud computing'.

These records connect each of us to each other.

The director knows your karma from past lives and helps you to deal with any karma you bring into this life. Your director is the divine mind.

Kevin J Todeschi sees the divine mind as "an unbiased judge and jury that attempt to guide, educate and transform every individual to become the best that he or she can be."

Karma is the universal law of cause and effect. Whatever positive and negative thoughts and actions we send out, circle back. This is akin to a boomerang!

Our director attempts to clear karmic energy blocks that can stop you from moving forward in this life.

Jennifer Gray, "it's like sowing and reaping. If you plant love and kindness, you shall get back in return."

Karma connects the past you, to the present you, and to the future you. They are all connected.

Kevin J Todeschi, "the successful meeting of karmic memory involves coming up with new resources and new modes of behavior" by your director.

Your director is aware of your positive and negative karma and sculpts it into your script in mystical ways, through coincidence, serendipitously, random meetings, etc.

You have not seen your best yet.
Prepare yourself to experience the
unexpected.
Life has mysterious ways.

SANGEETA RANA

EVERYTHING YOU HAVE EXPERIENCED HAS LED TO THIS MOMENT. Your director is aware of every action and reaction in your script.

The 'all-knowing' director of your life is your higher self, your soul, the divine mind, the universe.

Deepak Chopra, "there is no extra pieces in the universe. Everyone is here because he/she has a place to fill, and every piece must fit itself into the big jigsaw puzzle."

The universe knows each script. Each script connects to the universal script. Each script was designed to fit into the jigsaw puzzle of life.

Each soul on the world stage is moving forward into our collective future, all evolving with each script's unique design.

The ultimate 'line of communication' is for the director and the actor to be in a still space.

With meditation comes complete openness and freedom from the burdens of life. In your quiet space, you experience, in Deepak Chopra's words, your "pure potential being."

Your director is your pure potential being, expanding awareness.

Kevin J Todeschi, "prayer is talking to the divine, meditation is listening to the divine within."

Your director rolls the camera.

The mask and scene changes represent your experiences on your life's journey.

During meditation, a sacred space is created. In this divine space, your connection to the unlimited power and creativity of the universal script is aligned.

We all have set habits and routines that we have developed over time. We each have a self and a story that propels us through the day.

Through meditation, we are reconnected to our purpose, our script. Part of being renewed is the receptivity to a mask and scene change.

New situations, new experiences aligned to our script excite and exhilarate us.

Instead of recoiling from them, we engage in the new.

After 'still time', we feel re-energized, ready to go, and eager to meet each new challenge presented.

> *On our own, we cannot end wars or wipe out injustice, but the cumulative impact of thousands of 'small acts of goodness' can be bigger than we imagine.*
>
> QUEEN ELIZABETH II

SPECIAL EFFECTS
FROM YOUR
DIRECTOR

Signs

At any moment
You have a choice,
That either leads you closer
To your spirit
Or further away.

THICH NHAT HANH

SYMBOLS ARE THE CLUES WE SEEK TO FOLLOW OUR script.

Observing symbols or signposts in your day are subtle ways your director uses to guide you without disturbing the 'free will' expression of your life's script.

When in doubt about which way to proceed or not, look around for visible clues to assist you in your decision-making.

Robert Schuller, "problems are not stop signs. They are guidelines."

Sometimes your cue, symbol, or signpost can appear in human form, or a sign from nature (a snowstorm or weather condition that makes it impossible or dangerous to proceed), a thing (a traffic sign), or an animal, insect, or sign from nature.

Bernie Siegel, "a rainbow is a universal symbol of hope and life."

A rainbow makes everyone stop, look, and smile. It is a positive sign from your director.

Many markers will encourage you to take a certain path when you become attuned to the present moment.

THE ROAD NOT TAKEN

Two roads diverged in a yellow wood,
And sorry I could not travel both

ROBERT FROST

THE UNIVERSE WILL ACCOMMODATE YOUR DECISION.

Bernie Siegal, "survivors which, we all are don't have failures, they have delays or redirections."

There are few wrong decisions, maybe respites or roundabouts.

All roads, over time, lead to the completion of your lesson.

Your signposts are there each day for you. By remaining open, you allow the gentle winds of the universe to direct and redirect you.

Walter Isaacson, "one mark of a great mind is the willingness to change it."

Each day brings more special effects that are created for you.

Each special effect is hand-crafted to support your script.

Each sign is designed to raise the vibration of the universal stage you chose to be on.

Leo Tolstoy, "everyone thinks of changing the world, but no one thinks of changing himself."

The signs, each day, are written into your script to guide you.

The markers may lead to mask and scene changes.

All for your evolution on the world stage.

I have just three things to teach:
Simplicity, patience, compassion,
These three are your greatest treasures.

LAO TZU

Time

Deepak Chopra, "we say that the universe began with a bang, but actually, the early universe was more like a sky performance emerging from its dressing room. The early universe took its time until every seam fit together perfectly."

You are here only for a certain amount of time.

Your life journey is like the flow of a river. There are calm days when everything seems to move along nicely. Then there are stormy days when you wonder how will this end or where is this going?

Michael Singer, "all things with time, the energy will shift."

With this shift, one moves from stormy waters to calmer waters, and with this time, to rest your paddle and reflect.

Our timeline is from birth to death. For some short, for others longer, according to your script.

The 'way' is between birth and death.

Joseph Murphy, "the infinite mind is timeless and spaceless."

Your journey is infinite; if a lesson is postponed until the next life, that is acceptable.

Leo Tolstoy, "the two most powerful warriors are time and patience."

In the universe, there is no time. Each journey is one long continuum with your director's wisdom and the universal script guiding you.

Deepak Chopra, "patience allows you to be content as well as to pause, wait, endure and allow things to unfold in their own way and to recognize a bigger picture is unfolding."

There is peace with knowing, if not now, then maybe later—an internal trust in the infinite script that you authored.

Deepak Chopra, "a life well lived is small gradual changes."

These minor adjustments sanction the transitioning of a mask and scene.

This is a 'blessed' ritual.

The new mask, over time, slowly evolves and is tailored for its designated time.

Through your imagination and time, you allow the universe to guide you along your journey.

There is an internal 'knowing' when you are in the right place physically and mentally.

Ralph Waldo Emerson, "there is guidance for each of us, and by lowly listening, we shall hear the right word", and be guided to the right scene at the precise time.

One must take time to create time.

Deepak Chopra, "we are ageless beings that grow in wisdom and spiritual fulfillment in each passing moment."

With time, patience and trust, we become wise, fulfilled beings.

Mark Twain, "wrinkles should merely reflect where the smiles had been."

The 'action' occurs when living in the NOW.

Deepak Chopra, "living in the present enables us to literally stop time."

The Hopi Native Americans live in Arizona. They have no words for time.

Einstein, "time is an illusion, it's flexible, nonlinear, and a 24-hour day is a hoax."

If we think of time as a timeline, it will simplify and uncomplicate our life.

Thich Nhat Hanh "the past is gone, the future is not here, and if we do not go back to ourselves in the present moment, we cannot be in touch with life."

Starting your day with a framework of where you are going, what you would like to accomplish within your day, is helpful.

Instruments of time measurement help to structure and organize our daily activities.

Buddha, "each morning we are born again. What we do today matters most."

Live your day with flexibility. Being flexible and, in Elizabeth Hay's words, 'crab-like', which she saw as "moving sideways and backward rather than straight on."

This life is a flow of events with a master plan, your script.

Albert Einstein, "brief is this existence, as a fleeting visit in a strange house. The path to be pursued is poorly lit by a flickering consciousness."

It is a journey with a light guiding each of us forward. Some days the light is brighter.

The seeker seeks the rays of the infinite light.

Finding time to meditate, to be still, supports your well-being. Each of us has a time that feels right.

It is during your 'still time' that the tools that you require to master your lesson will be made available to you.

Early child educators and primary teachers work with each child's developmental timeline. They often use the word 'yet' when a child is occupied with acquiring a cognitive or physical skill. They encourage the child to keep persevering, as it has not happened 'yet', but it will happen soon.

Joseph Murphy wrote:

> *Try to live in the day.*
> *NOW is the time.*
> *Your inner voice will guide you NOW.*
> *Peace is NOW.*
> *Healing is NOW.*
> *Strength is NOW.*
> *Love is NOW.*
> *Guidance is NOW.*

When you are focused, all that is important is the NOW.

Joseph Murphy, "time is the release of the image that we are channeling in at the exact right time. To live in the NOW is to facilitate the perfect timing of that release."

Think of your timeline as: past- NOW- future.

Joseph Murphy sees the past and future as thieves who rob you of the 'joy' of the NOW. He added, "count your blessings now and get rid of those two thieves."

By living in the NOW, you channel in the additives of your day.

These ingredients are a simple recipe from the universe that, with time and patience, will grow into infinite possibilities.

Joseph Murphy, "your harvest is ready now in your mind. Ready your mind to receive your good NOW without further postponement."

Everything is orchestrated for each script's success.

Living in the NOW is all that is required of you for this success.

WILLIAM SHAKESPEARE, "ALL THINGS BE READY IF the mind be so."

Nature and Change

Henry Ward Beecher, "nature is God's tongue."

Nature is our sanctuary; we bond with its harmony and vibration.

The scene and mask changes which nature offers connects us to ALL.

The nature mask is loving, soothing and prepares us for change.

Thich Nhat Hanh, "walk as though you are kissing the Earth with your feet."

Nature provides many settings where reconnection with your script can ensue.

I recall reading that Winston Churchill regarded Uganda as "Africa's pearl."

All your senses are activated; nature's bounties are scattered throughout Uganda.

I remember helping children in the mountains in north Uganda.

It had been a troubling scene. We were in a remote area. The children were very needy. Our site was on the grounds of a local church. We were told that many families would send their children to the safety of the church at night.

We noticed across the path that only boys were playing in the field. We questioned where the girls were. Eyes went to the ground, as female circumcision occurs in some areas.

When presented with such information, one pauses and internally blesses all the darkness.

The team was somber for the rest of the deliveries and tried to linger with each child.

After the site, it was a quiet ride in the van. We stopped to visit Sipi Falls. We walked into the bush and followed a trail to the waterfalls.

Nature and all its 'magic' greeted our team on that trail. The children's sadness did not leave, but the beauty of Sipi Falls helped to distract us.

It was a 'pause' on life's journey.

A chance to reflect, to feel humbled by nature's beauty, and to 'bless' the role each child was playing on the world stage.

> *But there are lessons taught down there,*
> *I want this child to learn.*

EDGAR GUEST

What I saw, heard, and witnessed that day is embedded deep in my psyche.

Nature is our, 'whisperer'.

Nature welcomes the seeker and whispers its wisdom to all our senses.

Bernie Siegel, "if you watch how nature deals with adversity, continually renewing itself, you can't help but learn."

Nature offers the space, sometimes needed, to re-evaluate the scene you are in and the mask you are wearing.

Nature provides 'a re-connection to the womb' feeling.

Deepak Chopra, "our ancestral roots began in nature." He continued, "the sounds of nature are like an ancient drum."

Nature designs the stage to flow into a 'stillness space'. Here, one can reconnect with all of nature's gifts and wisdoms.

Marcus Aurelius, "dwell on the beauty of life. Watch the stars and see yourself running with them."

Nepal is known for its night sky beauty. On a clear night, 1500 stars glimmer.

We were visiting Pokhara, a city on Phewa Lake, in central Nepal. Pokhara is the 'gateway' to the Himalayan range.

One morning we woke before dawn and drove to Sarangkot to watch the sunrise over the Himalayan Mountains. Here we witnessed the first rays of sun contact the mountains and create an 'out of this world' rainbow of pastel illuminations—an 'awe' moment.

I had many experiences with the majestic Himalayan Mountains. This included a mountain flight over the Himalayan Mountains. The plane and the few passengers on board were all so small relative to the massive structures outside our plane's window.

The pilot and copilot allowed each passenger into the cockpit for a closer view of the Himalayans.

When my turn came, we were flying directly towards Mount Everest. We were so close; I could see the wind blowing the snow across the peak. It was a clear morning at the peak of Mt. Everest. The sun was shining brightly. There was a strong 'connection'.

When I returned to Canada, I tried to explain that connection; the words never came.

I visited the McMichael Art Gallery in the Toronto area. I saw Lauren Harris's painting, Abstraction. Abstraction was a mirror of Mount Everest's peak.

Once more no words, but now my vision was strengthened. I often visit the gallery and consider Abstraction to be a friend.

Nature teaches 'change'.

Octavia E Butler, "seed to tree, tree to forest, rain to river, river to sea, grubs to bees, bees to swarm. From one, many, from many one. Forever uniting, growing, dissolving, forever changing."

In Canada we experience the four seasons. Each season generates a new 'me'. The light changes inside and outside of me with each of the seasons.

Robert Delaunay, the "light in nature creates the movement of colors."

Each season, each day, is unique, a new beginning.

Heraclitus, "life is flux. Everything is constantly shifting and becoming something other to what it was before."

Nature is our master teacher, constantly nudging, "change is progress."

Heraclitus, "there is nothing permanent except change. If we can learn to handle this constant flux, we can handle life itself. Accept that everything is constantly changing and fleeting."

While in Uganda, I had the opportunity to visit Queen Elizabeth National Park. The Park is in west Uganda. It is known for its wildlife (African elephant, African buffalo, hippopotamus, leopard, lion, and over 500 species of birds).

During a boat ride along the Kazinga Channel, we noticed a harmonious site on the shore. The channel connects Lake George to Lake Edward.

Wilfrid Sellars, "to live happily with nature, we have to live in harmony with it."

A water buffalo, Nile crocodile, and elephant were all basking in the sun alongside each other. Our guide relayed that midday was 'quiet time'. It was the hottest time of day, and the animals just rested and were in harmony with their environment.

The day previously, our guide had gone off trail so we could witness five tree-climbing lions, also known as cactus climbing lions, relaxing in the heat of the mid-day sun on the branches of an acacia tree.

We quickly felt the vibration of the park. Its natural beauty was transformative.

Virginia Woolf, "a self that goes on changing is a self that goes on living."

When living in harmony with nature, change is welcomed.

Nature provides the space for a journey in, a connection with ALL.

Buddhism awakens the idea of "feeling compassion for ALL living things."

All things living that you encounter in your day are orchestrated by your internal director.

John Muir, "going out in nature and feeling all its magic is really going in."

Your journey in, connects with your true self.

Spending time in nature creates a natural bond between self and all life forms.

Anthony Doerr, "we rise again in nature."

Our team had many unsettling experiences while helping in Uganda.

Queen Elizabeth National Park in Uganda was a 'rebooting space.'

Nature flows seamlessly into new and novel ways of being. Each day a 'wonder,' a delight for our senses.

Another 'wonder,' while in Queen Elizabeth Park, was a chance meeting with a herd or a parade of elephants. We were driving and our guide suddenly stopped our vehicle.

He motioned for us to leave the off-roader, be quiet, and slowly move away from the jeep.

Shortly after, out of the bush came an enormous elephant. She stopped and used her trunk to sniff and to feel our vibration.

Our tracker did not have a weapon.

After several minutes she raised her trunk and trumpeted. Out of the bush came her herd. There were ten elephants and four babies who passed in front of us. The babies were holding onto their mother's tails with their small trunks.

At the very end of the procession was a very wobbly baby elephant. Our guide confirmed the wet baby elephant had just been born.

We had two more encounters during our stay with the matriarch of the elephant herd. One was at night. We were with our guide. Our accommodations were located on a high hill with a water hole below. There was a beautiful sunset. I could make out many animals in the waterhole. I noticed the elephant. Our guide confirmed it was the matriarch.

The day we left Queen Elizabeth Park, as we were driving out, there was our matriarch. Our guide said she came to say farewell.

The scenes from Queen Elizabeth Park sanctioned space to honor the lives of the Ugandan children, their families and to witness their contributions to the world stage. They 'highlighted' the simplicity of their lives.

The nature of Uganda shared its healing powers, the power of change and harmony among all living things.

I have had two other personal experiences with elephants. They were both in India. One in Kerala where I rode an elephant. I could feel every muscle moving and felt our hearts unite.

The next in Madurai in south India, at the Hindu temple. I visited this temple several times, and on reflection I believe the elephant's vibration called me.

Being in nature and connected to its 'all-knowing' vibration allows you to be at one with nature's innovative and resourceful energy.

Nature heals; so many plants have healing powers. I witnessed this when spending time with the local witch doctor. He simply walked into nature and returned with nature's 'magic' for the villager in need.

Charles Darwin, "it is not the strongest of the species that survive, not the most intelligent, but the one most responsive to change."

When my father died suddenly, we were devastated. He and my mother had both retired to take care of our two sons and my sister's three sons.

My parents were a terrific team; they took the boys to school, brought their grandsons home for lunch, transported each to their after-school activities, and played soccer with them on the driveway.

The first night after my dad's death, I could not sleep. I got up out of bed, dressed, went into the garage, and found my bike.

I rode my bike up and down the streets for the rest of the night. It was the trees that comforted me. We silently communicated as I continued to ride my bike. They soothed me, as we knew change was coming.

To this day, whenever I feel distressed, I seek out nature.

In Nepal, we were helping to bring water to a village in southwest Nepal.

Nepal was still recovering from a 2015 devastating earthquake. The highway we traveled on for 13 hours had been severely affected by the earthquake. They were slowly rebuilding it.

This was all washed away by the stunning scenery, the swaying rope bridges over deep valleys, and the smiles on the Nepalese people.

Our accommodations were at a farm homestay close to Chitwan.

On the last day, we went for a hike. We walked out of the homestay, and in less than 15 minutes, we were in Chitwan National Park, also known as The Heart of the Jungle.

On our first night in Madi, our hosts entertained the team with music and dance. Our main guide was an elderly, kind man. I had met him there and was so relieved to know he was leading our trek.

All guides only carried a stick, no weapons, which I resonated with.

When asked what to do if a rhino charged at us, he pointed to a nearby tree and said, "climb." This was all translated to the team.

Chitwan has a variety of big animals, which include rhinos, Bengal tigers, Indian leopards, snakes, and an abundance of species of birds.

It was a tranquil walk. I walked at the back of the group. I enjoyed the silence; the pace allowed me to connect with the vibration of Chitwan. We were walking in tall grass, and I just had this feeling there was a presence to the right of me. Just that 'knowing' feeling.

I connected to the many sounds and felt at one with the environment which I was now part of. Slowly we moved out of the tall grass, and I could see the team was gathering around something.

When I approached, I saw the fresh footprint of a tiger. Oh my, I thought, was that the presence I felt?

As we trekked, we saw many streams. Our guides were obviously the custodians of Chitwan. When seeing any small dam that had formed in the rivers, they gently unclogged them.

As we were about to descend a steep embankment, I noticed several team members glancing at an area with an indentation in the sandy soil of a HUGE snake's body. We were told that the snake had heard us coming and had either slithered away into the underbrush or into the stream which we were about to cross. As we wadded across the shallow stream, we all hoped not to encounter the snake.

We eventually approached a ranger station. We rested and chatted. The head guide gathered us together and pulled a young tree from his backpack. He asked ME to plant it. I was shocked, "me?"

I took the sapling in my hands. As I was about to plant it, he told me this was for my grandson.

I looked at him; there was a 'connection'. He did not know I was about to become a Nain for the first time, our new grand-child a boy. At first surprise and then just a 'knowing' feeling. Of course, he would know!

Martin Luther King Jr., "I saw God. I saw him in the birds of the air, the leaves of the tree, the movement of the rippling waves. Sometimes I go out at night and look at the stars as they bedeck the heavens like shining silver pins sticking in a magnif-icent blue pin cushion. There is God. Sometimes I watch the moon as it walks across the sky as a queen walks across her masterly mansion."

We witness the power of nature when we see a plant growing in a cement path; it is determined to find the 'light'.

Richard Burton, there is "powerful medicine that comes from physically connecting with plants growing and expanding and is our master teacher."

I recall reading in an article that France at one time had a brutal prison colony located on the islands of French Guiana. Once the prison was abandoned, nature had slowly trans-formed this very dark place into a tropical paradise with nature's 'magical' light. Perhaps the message is that with time, nature's light prevails.

Henry David Thoreau, "an early morning walk is a blessing for the whole day."

Nature is healthier than taking a sedative.

Nature is here to teach, inspire, and comfort.

Martin Luther King Jr. felt to "commune with nature" is a lifeline.

I felt and saw this lifeline with my mom. I recall her sitting in a wheelchair outside. We were in a hurry.

I remember her saying, "please, I just want to feel the breeze."

I often think of that scene when I am rushing. The older I become, there is an understanding of where my mom was. She knew she was in one of her last scenes. She just wanted to pause.

She knew the next scene was coming, her last mask change.

Walt Whitman, "I believe a blade of grass is not less than the journey work of the stars."

Nature allows you to enter the realm of infinite possibilities. Nature is constantly growing, changing, and expanding and is a gentle guide.

Another adventure, I recall, occurred after helping children in Jinja on Lake Victoria's north shore.

We boarded a primitive boat and headed out into Lake Victoria. We were told we were going to see the source of the Nile.

We passed several local fishermen in their dug-out wooden boats. They were tending to their nets and the catches of their day.

After a short distance, we circled bubbling water, which had surfaced from the depths of Lake Victoria. As I put my hand into the bubbly water, I thought of the water's journey from the mountains to here and beyond. And of ALL the creative paths mother nature facilitates for each of us.

Deepak Chopra, "connecting with nature is for us to witness the dance of the universe and to see us as part of this magnificent symphony."

Wherever I am, I have a connection not only to nature but also to the people of that area. I can feel this connection, but words escape me.

Wade Davis is an anthropologist. Through his travels and research, he successfully put into words the connections I experienced in my travels.

Davis, "the sum total of all thoughts, intuitions, myths and beliefs, ideas and inspirations brought into being by the human imagination since the dawn of consciousness" are present in what Davis calls the 'ethnosphere'.

He continues, "just as there is a biological web of life known as the biosphere, there exists a cultural fabric of existence that connects on earth."

While hiking in Uganda we met several displaced Batwa pygmies. They had once lived in their ancestral Bwindi Forest. The forest provided for all their needs. They lived alongside the mountain gorillas. Their dislocation and adjustment to a new environment was causing them much distress. Their population was dwindling due to the 'disconnect' with their ethnosphere.

Walter Isaacson felt that Einstein believed "math is the language nature uses to describe her wonders."

Is math nature's manual?

Walter Isaacson suggests Einstein could sniff out the underlying physical principles of nature. Einstein came to appreciate that math could be a tool for discovering nature's laws.

Deepak Chopra, "our health and well-being is connected to nature, and so it is up to us to enjoy all that it generously offers us each day."

Nature connects us to 'one'. Deepak Chopra, "the same energy that flows through nature is the same energy that connects us all together."

Oneness exceeds individuality. Oneness blends all people, creatures, and things of the world.

Albert Einstein, "a human being is part of the whole called by us universe, a part limited in time and space. We experience ourselves, our thoughts, and feelings as something separate from the rest. A kind of optical delusion of consciousness. This delusion is a kind of prison for us, restricting us to our personal desires and to affection for a few persons nearest to us. Our task must be to free ourselves from the prison by widening our circle of compassion to embrace all living creatures and the whole of nature in its beauty. The true value of a human being is determined primarily by the measure and the sense in which they have obtained liberation from the self. We shall require a substantially new manner of thinking if humanity is to survive."

I experienced Einstein's 'thinking' when gorilla trekking in Bwindi.

I was in a small group. We walked through thick, sinking underbrush for about four hours before joining our family of 28 gorillas.

Our family of gorillas consisted of 2 silverbacks (unusual) and several babies who were on their mother's backs. We walked with the gorillas as they traveled through their day.

Our guides told us to avoid looking into the eyes of the gorillas. I followed their instructions for a while, then slowly feeling the connection raised my gaze. I felt the gorillas had adopted me. Seeing these regal creatures in their natural habitat was sheer joy.

There is a humorous story that happened on our gorilla trek. Two members of the group were from the southern US. They were not dressed for such an arduous trek. I liked them immediately and after a few chats, discovered they were bird watchers. They were on the trek for the birds, not the gorillas.

Each of nature's parts has a specific message for each of us.

Bernie Siegel, "a butterfly is a symbol of transformation."

Nature has been my vehicle for my journey in. Nature has been relentlessly patient with me. She has been my other mother and has guided me in my internal awareness expansion. She has materialized scenes and mask changes for me that have enriched my experiences in this lifetime.

One such scene was the red clay in Uganda. We were on our way to helping children. It was raining 'buckets'. We were in a small van and traveling along rural back roads. Due to the pouring rain, our van got stuck. We knew the children were waiting.

We decided to walk the rest of the way to the site. The red clay was thick on the soles of our shoes. We took them off, and the feeling of the red clay against bare skin still lingers in my fondest memories. We arrived at the site and delivered the supplies to the children.

We then headed back to the van, still barefoot. This time our journey was slower. I was towards the back with the younger children who had received their supplies. I was helping them carry their new things. They were helping me stay upright on the slippery red clay. One child found me a tall stick to help me walk. We must have looked a sight.

At some point I looked up to discover we were alone—no one in sight. I just continued with the children. Laughing and slipping along. Parents eventually started arriving to meet their children. They could see I was lost and accompanied me to the now unstuck van. I love remembering this story. It puts a smile on my face.

Lao Tzu, "accept what is in front of you, without wanting the situation to be other than it is. Nature provides everything without requiring thanks and provides for all."

While in Kolkata, we visited the museum. I was wandering through the vast rooms and noticed a simple rosary in a glass cabinet.

Each part of the rosary was from nature. It had belonged to Mother Teresa.

Leave the road,
take the trails.

PYTHAGORAS

Creativity

Robert Bresson, "make visible what, without you, might perhaps never have been seen."

Each of us has a creative mask. Our creative mask connects the mask wearer to the infinite creative powers of the universe.

Deepak Chopra sees creativity as, "the light of our creative self is our most precious gift to the world as it unites, heals, and uplifts everyone it reaches."

Creativity creates a path to becoming unstuck. A path to seeing things differently. A path to new mask and scene changes.

Your creative mask allows you to see the 'wonders' of your world.

Maya Angelo felt creativity was limitless, "the more you use it, the more you have."

Our director, our higher self, seeks to evolve through creativity.

Creativity, to Deepak Chopra, is a "spontaneous expression of our innermost desires and intentions. The power of our intention directs our life journey behind the scenes."

Each creative act has different scenes incorporated into your script.

Your creative mask channels in new ideas, thoughts, and behaviors. These ideas are unique. They bring with them new inspirations, new vibrant colors for the world stage.

Criss Jami, "create with the heart, build with the mind."

Your creativity mask prompts you to see 'connections'.

Sam Horn, "creativity is simply connecting new dots in new ways."

New thoughts and ideas resemble, in Julia Cameron's words, "spiritual electricity." They energize the connector with the souls who are ready to receive this new current from the universe.

Deepak Chopra, "what keeps life fascinating is the constant creativity of the soul."

A child's creative mask is their innate mode of expression. As an educator, I witnessed creativity in every child I taught. Teachers attempt to recognize, support, and nurture each child's creative gifts.

Francesca Gino, children have a "sense of wonder crucial to creativity and innovation."

Each child's creative mask is their statement, their interpretation of their world. Children flow with their creativity. Their creativity appears effortless, free of any inhibitions.

Einstein, "creativity is intelligence having fun."

I used to love setting up creative centers for students and my own children. I attempted to include the materials they would need to express themselves freely. An environment where there was no competition, just free expression and exploration. Each center was facilitated with the creativity of the child in mind. Their enthusiasm and mine blended into one. I marveled at all their creations.

I taught and tried to incorporate into our classroom and home that "life is about using the whole box of crayons."

Your creative mask sometimes becomes soiled as life's journey takes you down many different paths.

Pablo Picasso, "art wastes away from the soul the dust of everyday life."

You have many gifts, which are expressed through your creative mask. Creativity channels from a 'showcase of curiosities' which nurtures your soul.

Brenda Ueland, "everybody is talented because everybody, who is human, has something to express."

To have time to ponder, to be still, is providing the space for your creative mask to transition on.

Each day, take time to daydream, imagine the new possibilities, the wonders of the world stage. Immerse your imagination, fantasy, and dreams into your reality.

Deepak Chopra, "through meditation, we expand our awareness. We align our intentions with the unlimited creativity of the universal mind and create a creative path."

We are not on a solitary journey.

Our creative gifts are for ALL on the world stage.

Each creative gift contributes to our evolution.

I have recently concluded that the best psychiatrist is your own 'inner creativity'.

BRENE BROWN, "CREATIVITY IS THE WAY I SHARE MY soul with the world."

Curiosity

ALBERT EINSTEIN, "I AM NEITHER CLEVER NOR especially gifted. I am only very, very curious. I have no special talents. I am only passionately curious."

Curiosity is the desire to know more about anything. This involves observing and questioning, followed by creative solutions.

An example of Einstein's curiosity is found in Walter Isaacson's book Einstein:

Einstein's son asks his father, "why are you so famous?"

Einstein answered, "when a blind beetle crawls over the curved branch, it doesn't notice that the track it has covered is indeed curved. I was lucky enough to notice what the beetle didn't notice."

As an educator, I appreciate children's flow of questions and the divergent creative styles used to discover answers.

Each classroom teacher has an assigned curriculum to follow. It provides a teacher with a framework, but within that blueprint, most teachers establish an inquiry model.

Gino, "children have an insatiable need to understand the world around them."

Teachers often ask the questions: Why? How? What if? And have the tools available for their students to explore potential answers.

Children like to talk, observe, touch, question results, explore freely and take risks.

Einstein, "it is a miracle that curiosity survives formal education."

Children survive when given an inquiry model which will last a lifetime. Many inventions, new thoughts, and ideas throughout our history result from curiosity and its twin mask creativity.

Gino, "teachers nurture curiosity which fuel learning and discovery."

The schoolroom, home, and nature provide limitless possibilities to the child for free exploration to broaden their interests.

Einstein, "the important thing is not to stop questioning. Curiosity has its own reason for existing."

Curiosity can lead to exploring unknown paths, which excites the seeker.

Curiosity involves observing and inquiring. The questions one asks makes one active in the pursuit of new discoveries.

Einstein, "curiosity is more important than knowledge."

While helping in Nepal, we stayed for several nights in Kathmandu. One afternoon, we sat outside having a mug of chia tea at a local teahouse.

I was seated, facing a very unsafe construction site. I became very curious as I watched two women, each with a basket strung to their back and head, walk up and down six outdoor flights of dangerous crumbling steps: no safety railings, no safety precautions of any kind.

We approached the women. We saw them each load the other's basket with red bricks. They then carried the full baskets up the stairs, unloaded the bricks and descended with construction debris in their baskets.

We never saw them take a break. Our waiter spoke English. We asked him to ask the two middle-aged sisters, "what could we do to help them?"

All they wanted was a chicken dinner from the nearby restaurant. As the food arrived, they sparingly ate a bit and wrapped the remainder for their families to finish when they returned home.

We watched as they loaded up each other's basket and continued their upward trek.

Our curiosity initiated this learning situation for us and our introduction to these two non-complaining superwomen.

I silently blessed their journey and their role on the world stage.

Curiosity arouses, it encourages and excites one to go out and explore the world.

Curiosity engages you actively as you use each sense to search out potential answers.

Your curiosity mask is a gift you brought in with you from the universe. It has the potential to lead to a global seeker.

Gino "the impulse to seek new information and experiences and explore novel possibilities is a basic human attribute."

The mind is a muscle, and the mental exercise triggered by curiosity makes your mind stronger.

Curiosity's desire for information and the journey this involves can create possible scenes for mask changes.

Einstein, "success comes from curiosity, concentration, perseverance, and self-criticism."

A life journey of seeking is asking questions and the quest for the answers.

Curiosity can create uncertainty. This can be unsettling, but with perseverance and determination, the seeker in you eventually will find the answer, your 'pot of gold'.

Gino, "when we are curious, we view tough situations more creatively."

And with that, the creativity mask transitions on with creative solutions.

Walt Disney, "we keep moving forward, opening new doors, and trying new things, because we are curious, and curiosity keeps leading us down new paths."

Music and Dance

Dick Clark, "music is the soundtrack of your life."

Your musical mask is on a shelf in your storeroom of masks. You may reach for it, frequently.

Plato, "music and rhythm find their way into the secret place of the soul."

Your musical mask transitions you into an open space.

Elizabeth Hay, "sound can influence your mood." Sometimes there is "sound without a source. It can cause a spontaneous humming or movement that just seemed to come from nowhere."

Music creates a channel, connecting you to a vibration that you are seeking.

Louis Armstrong, "music is life itself."

Music sets the stage for a communion with your purpose. It is a 'rally call'; it connects you to messages from the universe.

The soundtrack from Chariots of Fire was my call.

Chariots of Fire is a 1981 British historical film. It is based on the story of athletes in the 1924 Olympics.

Vangelis wrote and recorded Chariots of Fire's instrumental soundtrack. Music, to Vangelis, is "one of the greatest forces in the universe."

The vibration from Chariots of Fire's musical score 'struck a chord'. I felt the strength of spirit over form.

It was my 'spiritual call' and elevated my vibration.

Plato, "music gives a soul to the universe, wings to the mind, flight to the imagination and life to everything."

Your musical mask can be a passage to your still space, where union with your higher self can ensue.

Aldous Huxley, "after silence, that which comes nearest to expressing the inexpressible is music."

For several summers, we rented a well-worn beach house on a quiet rocky small beach in Maine. It was 'spot-on' for our two active and often sand-covered children.

The waves lulled me to sleep most nights. The ocean was my evening lullaby.

Alan Gratz, "the ringing of the sea, the singing lullaby of it."

Alan Gratz saw each journey as a song, each passage as a verse.

Music often leads to dance. Alan Gratz, "you can live as a ghost waiting for death, or you can dance."

Music and dance each have the potential to raise your vibration.

Lao Tzu, "music in the soul can be heard by the universe."

Music is a universal mask worn throughout time.

I have personally enjoyed a variety of music during my journey. I have reached for my musical mask throughout my life. Now, classical music summons me.

Music creates a space where I can release suppressed emotions that were difficult to free.

Debasish Mridha, "music can heal the soul that medicine cannot touch."

Music is a unique art form using sound.

Johann Sebastian Bach, "music is an agreeable harmony for the honor of God and the permissible delights of the soul."

I like to dance as well. When I taught primary education, we danced and sang daily. Once I retired less so, until I began to help in developing countries.

Cuba is music. My mother lived in Santiago de Cuba for six months each year. When I visited her, music and dance were everywhere, inside and outside homes.

Einstein, "if I were not a physicist, I would probably be a musician. I often think in music. I see my life in terms of music."

In Uganda, we often danced. The local musicians expressed their gratitude by performing with their homemade instruments. They would play and we would all dance, children included.

Henry Wadsworth Longfellow, "music is the universal language of mankind."

In the Philippines, we celebrated with karaoke. Most nights we sang old favorite songs and danced.

Hans Christian Anderson, "where words fail, music speaks."

I witnessed this connection in Africa, India, the Philippines, Cuba, and Nepal. Language was not a barrier, as music and dance filled the void.

Heinrich Heine, "where words leave off, music begins."

Thinking back, I recall walking with a botanist in south India. We were in a rural area. We hiked up and down a steep hill. He would patiently enlighten us about each plant's 'magic'. As we approached the path at the bottom of the slope, we noticed a small group of motorists who had stopped. They were all gazing up the hill. We had just descended. We joined them. I could hear loud thrashing and bumping sounds. When I focused in, on all the movement and sound, I saw two giant cobras. I was told they were performing a 'courtship dance'.

I remember thinking at the time, everything and everyone loves to dance.

Every disease is a musical problem,
Every cure is a musical solution.

NOVALIS

Books

Susan Orlean, "books have souls."

How often have you started a book and had the feeling there was at least one message in it specifically for you?

A book is a 'treasure'. I feel so fortunate that I have the skill to read. It is a gift that I honor.

Barack Obama, "reading is the gateway skill that makes all other learning possible."

Each book contains a unique pearl for everyone.

Virginia Woolf, "books are the mirrors of the soul."

Books stretch each of us. Our perspectives are broadened; we become open to new thoughts, ideas, and other worlds.

~

Let us remember:
One book,
One pen,
One child,
One teacher,
Can change the world.

MALALA YOUSAFZAI

Books present us with 'what if' questions. Through the author's words, we can be transformed into different spaces, cultures, occupations, and assorted vistas.

Sometimes in life, we have to stay put for various reasons. Covid-19 was one reason.

Mason Cooley, "reading gives someplace to go when we have to stay where we are."

Most individuals have periods of 'loneliness'. In these times, a book can be a friend, a therapist, and soul mate.

Dan Brown, "time is a river, and books are boats."

In my life, a book appears at the exact right time for my inner growth and outward expansion. It can be a word, a simple sentence, a paragraph, a verse, or a picture—each re-igniting something deep within me.

The more that you read,
The more things you will know.
The more that you learn,
The more places you'll go.

DR. SEUSS

. . .

WHEN I READ, I HAVE A SEPARATE BOOK JOURNAL. I log words, quotes, thoughts that I can reflect on at the right time. Sometimes the fitting time can be days, months, and years ahead.

Henry David Thoreau, "books are the treasured wealth of the world."

When in Kampala I helped in a local school. The school was so proud of the one shelf in a shell of a room called the library. The one narrow, short shelf had all the books for the entire school. Each of those books was a 'treasure' to each student and to each teacher.

Write to be understood,
Speak to be heard
Read to grow.

LAWRENCE CLARK POWELL

As an educator, I see the world expanding when a child learns to read.

Reading is a 'miracle'. I am aware of all the skills required to learn to read, which must be mastered.

An ideal enhancing environment is one that is rich in music, books, and conversation. This model space can nurture the 'love of reading'.

Mary Ellen Chase, "there is no substitute for books in the life of a child."

Books can be transformative. Each book in the bibliography of All The World Is A Stage expanded my awareness. Each author extended my 'openness'.

Most books have an intention and can take you on a journey within and outside of yourself.

FREDERICK DOUGLASS, "ONCE YOU LEARN TO READ, you will be forever free."

Friends (Support Actors)

ANAIS NIN, "EACH FRIEND REPRESENTS A WORLD IN us, a world possibly not born until they arrive, and it is only by this meeting that a new world is born."

Friends are sacred and should be cherished and appreciated. They are often your earth angels and in your life for a reason.

Well-wishers are like circling planets, approaching for an exchange of energy.

Carl Jung, "the meeting of two personalities is like the contact of two chemical substances: if there is any reaction, both are transformed."

Each encounter has been meticulously planned and scripted for each participant to benefit from this meeting.

Deepak Chopra, "I cherish my every connection."

Each friend, each acquaintance, is in your script. Many are your support actors, collaborating with you on the world stage.

Deepak Chopra, "I see that my pure awareness also exists in others."

Often one experiences that feeling of 'I was just thinking of you'. And surprise, an email, text, phone call, or a direct encounter occurs.

Are these chance meetings, or was it simply meant to be?

Jen Sincero "be with people whose energy lights you up."

When the scene is completed, the individuals return to their respective journeys. There may or may not be another encounter.

Deepak Chopra, "we are social creatures who thrive in communities. Connecting with one another allows us to express our most heartfelt hopes and dreams and to be of service to one another. Our supportive relationships enhance the positive messages we send our bodies each day, inviting greater health and well-being into our lives."

Friends can 'shore up' your script. It can be as simple as a word, a gesture, an action that will trigger something deep inside of you to propel you forward.

Jen Sincero, "the people you surround yourself with are excellent mirrors for who you are and how much, or how little, you love yourself."

Sometimes you may experience negative feelings toward an individual. It will not always be a pleasant scene. However, know there are no accidents. There is a reason for encountering this person at this precise moment in your life.

This friend might share a thought or idea with you, a potential seed. Few things are random. That seed has the potential to flourish into an 'enlightening' inspiration that could thrust you and this dimension onward. Everything and everyone has the capacity to enrich the world stage!

Deepak Chopra, "be grateful for the many individuals who contribute to your life and in whose lives, you make a difference."

When the friendship wanes, it is the wise soul that celebrates the union and sanctions the friend to move on in the direction they should travel, to move forward on their journey.

Eleanor Roosevelt, "many people will walk in and out of your life, but only true friends will leave footprints in your heart."

The ebb and flow of friendships are constant, and there is a rhythm to it, like the universal dance.

When a friend moves on, wish them well and envision wings for them to fly with, as they have served you well. You are a better soul for their brief or lengthy stay in your life.

Sometimes friendships dissolve: negativity lingers, and through time one can see why that soul was in your life. Perhaps you both helped each other to master a lesson. When you are receptive to this philosophy, every day is an open book, an adventure.

ELEANOR ROOSEVELT, "FRIENDSHIP WITH ONESELF IS all important because, without it, one cannot be friends with anyone else in the world."

Miracles

RALPH WALDO EMERSON, "THE INVARIABLE MARK OF wisdom is to see the miraculous in the common."

When one is quiet and still, one can see and feel miracles.

Everyday miracles occur and are viewed by the individuals who have the time and curiosity, to observe them.

Birth is a miracle. An 'awe' moment.

Bernie Siegel, "a miracle comes quietly into the mind. That stops an instant and is still."

As a traveling helper, I witnessed miracles.

I recall helping give out supplies to needy children in an area in eastern Uganda.

We tended to have the sickly and younger children at the beginning and the older children towards the end.

I realized we were going to be short two supplies.

The last two recipients were two thin, lanky older boys. They had traveled far and were accompanied by the headmaster of their school. He spoke English. We asked him to explain to his two students the situation and that somehow, we would get their supplies to them.

I understood how this situation could happen as we are all helpers, but this did not diminish our promise to the boys.

Robert Schuller, "impossible situations can become possible miracles."

I recall the trust in each of the Ugandan boy's eyes when the situation was explained to them.

Bernie Siegel, "when one believes in love and miracles, divine intervention can occur."

At the very last site in western Uganda, we found the two missing provisions. But how to get them to the boys?

We were nearing the end of our day. I looked up to see the headmaster walking toward us. We were all so happy to see him and to pass on the supplies to those two trusting, deserving young boys. To us, that was our miracle, and I think the boy's miracle too.

Theodore Roosevelt, "believe you can, and you're halfway there."

On reflection, I just knew the boys would receive their supplies. I just did not know how.

At the end of another helping site in Uganda, we lingered with the children who had just received their supplies. Their energy and 'joy' were invigorating. We were walking back to our van, and in the nearby bush we could hear wailing.

I walked with my friend toward the disturbing sound. We found a young mother who was extremely upset, as her child had not received supplies. She explained that the chief of her village had given the supplies to another more deserving village child.

Her grief was overwhelming. She had traveled a distance to see what her child had not received.

We had an extra provision in the van. We consulted with the team members, who unanimously agreed her child should receive the supplies.

Bernie Siegal, "miracles occur where the invisible possibilities of life unfold as realities."

There is an understanding that comes with miracles. If you are open, positive, and believe in the universe's wisdom and that anything is possible, you are opening the door for a miracle to transition in.

BERNIE SIEGEL, "LIFE IS A MIRACLE, AND IT IS derived from the intelligent, loving conscious energy that created it."

DISTRACTIONS
FROM YOUR SCRIPT

Fear

Kyle Gray, "wherever love is, fear is a stranger."

Love is inherent in each of us; fear is a stranger that visits in unwanted ways and unsettles each of us in a different manner.

Tom Friedman, "nothing in life is to be feared, it is only to be understood. Now is the time to understand more so that we may fear less."

Your role on the world stage encounters fear throughout its many scenes.

Jen Sincero, "focus on your desire, not fear."

When boarding a plane to help in a developing country, I generally experience an unsettling feeling. I recognize this sensation as 'fear'.

George Bernhard Shaw, "a life spent making mistakes is not only more honorable, but more useful than a life spent doing nothing."

I board the plane, find my seat, and prepare my new environment for a long flight. In due course, I look to my right and to my left. I start chatting with strangers, and eventually, my fear mask slowly fades. I move from fear and apprehension to my adventure mask.

Another successful mask shift has occurred.

Jen Sincero, "let fear be your compass."

From takeoff to my eventual return home, I try to acknowledge each fear that visits me.

Eleanor Roosevelt, "you gain strength, courage, and confidence by every experience in which you look fear in the face."

My mother was a seeker. I recall hosting a family dinner. My mother was present. I do not remember how the conversation began, but at one point my mother quietly said to her family, "my time in the Cuban jail was not as bad as my spell in the Columbian jail."

Those words stopped all conversations. I said, "mom, we didn't know this?" To which she just nodded.

After my dad's sudden death, my mom slowly transitioned into a global citizen. My mom was a private, humble woman. A woman of few words, but many actions. She had a hunger to understand life and pursued this in her later years internationally.

After this conversation, I was at an airport in south Cuba with my mom. We had just entered the airport and I heard in English, "Jennie, Jennie!" This was my mom's first name.

A young Cuban gentleman who worked at the airport rushed over and introduced himself to me. He explained, "he was the one who helped to arrange the release of my mom from the Cuban jail."

After boarding the plane, I asked my mom, "what the Cuban jail was like?" "OK, I complained that my cell was too hot. The nice jailor left the door open, so I could get fresh air. The food was OK as well", she added.

My mom met all her fears with humor and determination. She refused to allow fear to close any doors. My mother was in her late 70s and early 80s when her prison stays occurred.

Aung San Suu Kyi, "the only real prison is fear, and the only real freedom is freedom from fear."

When I struggle with fear, often a new awareness is preparing to surface from my inner world. Recently I was struggling with the limitations of the Covid virus on my family, friends, and the planet.

In my seventies, I was feeling like an 'endangered species'. My new awareness was to see the virus as a teacher. To respect the virus, not to fear it.

Plato, "courage is knowing what not to fear."

An 'entrance' opened for me with this awareness, the time to finish this book. I had started it almost twenty years ago.

Ralph Waldo Emerson, "in each pause I hear the call."

The virus became my teacher. Once I acknowledged this, I heard my call. I had transitioned from fear to respect for the virus.

There is magic if one sees each fear as a teachable opportunity. In the 'still space' where you meet your fear, utilize it as a sacred reflection time. Allow times of stagnation and contemplation to lead to a deeper and more meaningful summit with your fear.

Along my journey, I was presented with this understanding of fear:

F false

E expectations

A appear

R real

ON MY LIFE JOURNEY, THUS FAR, THIS UNDER-standing has facilitated 'carrying on'.

Einstein "no problem can be solved from the same level of consciousness that created it."

My dealings with fear required my journey in, my connection with my 'all-knowing' director, my reflection time.

In my space within, my higher self acknowledges the fear obstruction and nurtures creative solutions.

Michael Singer, "the purpose of spiritual evolution is to remove the blockages that cause your fear."

Snakes can create uneasy feelings for me. I avoided many scenes in my earlier years because of this fear. My intention not to close doors because of my fear of snakes has served me well.

Dr. Stephane Treyvaud, "trust that in the dark night of the soul, the safety of our true self will carry us. Removing fear allows grace to humbly begin the unendarkment."

Due to my gradual understanding of fear, the universe has, over the years, presented me with many scenes to challenge my anxiety of snakes.

I have grown from a teenager in Algonquin Park screaming and running from a garter snake to an elder who hiked through areas in Uganda, Rwanda, Nepal, Australia, and India with the full knowledge that I was in 'risky' snake terrain.

> *Come to the edge.*
> *We will fall*
> *Come to the edge.*
> *It's too high.*
> *COME TO THE EDGE!*
> *And they came,*
> *and he pushed,*
> *And they flew.*

> CHRISTOPHER LOGUE

I feel that push from the universe when I connect with each of my fears.

MICHEL DE MONTAIGNE, "HE WHO FEARS HE SHALL suffer, already suffers what he fears."

Ego

A bad day
For your ego
Is a great day
For your soul.

JILLIAN MICHAELS

CONFIDENCE OFTEN LEADS TO SUCCESS. WITH confidence, one is grateful for and acknowledges each unique gift that accompanies you from the universe. A confident person does not need to be recognized; inner harmony is their intention.

Ego can stifle or alter sacred gifts that are within you. Ego is false confidence and can lead to self-sabotage. Too much ego can diminish your talents, your gifts.

Ego emboldens feelings of entitlement. The need for external recognition and validation are signs of an inflated ego.

I understand EGO to be:

E energy

G going

O out

EGO CAN PREVENT YOU FROM HEARING CRITICAL information relevant to your life's journey. Ego is your 'talkative' lower self.

Einstein envisioned ego as "red tape encases the mind, like the hands of a mummy."

A newborn has no ego. They are egoless. They are pure energy with no 'red tape'. Newborns act solely on intuition and their immediate needs.

Deepak Chopra, "ego has insecurities, ego cannot reach true playfulness."

Ego can create a feeling of superiority, which is a detrimental belief.

Deepak Chopra, "ego is into winning and not losing."

As you expand, ego can tiptoe into your role on the world stage. The ego favors the material world and a flashy lifestyle. The ego likes the negative prizes that come with fame and fortune. Ego burrows in and becomes comfortable in the lower self, where it can govern.

Albert Einstein, "the intuitive mind is a secret gift and the rational mind a faithful servant."

Deepak Chopra, "society honors the servant and forgets the gift."

Society, through ego, can be comparable to 'big brother', forever trying to manipulate all your actions and thoughts.

Deepak Chopra, "ego is a confining place to live."

Ego is an unnatural state and can create feelings of depleted self-worth.

Over time, many individuals 'awaken' and begin questioning and challenging some of society's guidelines, branding, and protocols.

We ponder a different lifestyle.

Radhanath Swami, "surrender means surrender of your ego."

It is not the material world that fulfills us, but the gifts within each of us that bring us their many blessings.

I witness this every day when I am helping in developing countries. In many community spots, such as a well in southern India or a pond in northern India, souls are laughing and sharing what they have for the betterment of their humble community.

It is a memory that I carry with me when I return to a developed country where everyone appears, at times, to be out for themselves, and the feeling of community fades.

Deepak Chopra envisions ego as "pure selfishness."

Opportunities arise in many lives, for a mask shift to egoless.

Some develop an awareness of 'herd behavior'—people associating with a group rather than an independent philosophy.

Robert Louis Stevenson, "to know what you prefer, instead of humbly saying Amen to what the world tells you you ought to prefer, is to have kept your soul alive."

I recall being with a friend who remarked to me, "do you notice how many people are wearing the color black?" I did not until this was mentioned to me. I, too, was wearing black.

That statement came at the exact right time in my life; it was pivotal. I started noticing the 'sheep' phenomenon in my own life—the group movement, seldom elevating to see different perspectives.

Deepak Chopra, "they perform actions without regard to outcomes or fruits of actions."

From time to time, some choose to leave the 'group think' and begin their own self-reliant journey.

Deepak Chopra, "egoless is free and open."

The group will pursue the conscientious member and encourage them to return to the cluster. However, the mask transition has begun.

The ego begins the negative internal dialogue and attempts to sabotage the process.

Dr. Stephane Treyvaud, we "live in a narrative bubble, a cultural envelope of social norms, we mistake for reality."

The individual has seen other distinctive patterns and diverse ways of thinking which are beckoning.

Your openness evolves when parting from your 'comfort zone'.

Zen, "empty mind in order to become receptive to a new reality."

New scenes in your life script transition in.

Deepak Chopra, "self-importance can slow spiritual growth obscure your understanding of who you are. Seeking opportunities to limit ego creates space to enter your life. You return to your original self and see with your eyes, not the eyes of society and your ego. You have simply forgotten who you are. Awakening to the true self is gradual. Little by little, you release stress and limiting thought patterns that obscure your awareness of your essential nature, which is always there shining brightly."

Sometimes this can be a challenging transition.

Deepak Chopra, "if we feel like something is missing, it is because we are seeing through the ego-mind which has a limited perspective of our infinite nature."

This new mask and scene change can be uncomfortable, feelings of loneliness and isolation can enter your psyche.

With time your new mask and scene transition will generate new support, new environments, and a higher vibration, all being your reward for your 'stick-to-itiveness'.

This higher vibration will allow you to maximize the gifts you have brought into this dimension, making it a better place for ALL.

Mahatma Gandhi, "when the ego dies, the soul awakes."

With this new mask comes an awareness of egoless, a feeling of being comfortable in your own skin, your own body. You transition to having thicker skin, a trust in your innovative words and thoughts. You laugh at yourself more readily. Your heart opens. You have new feelings of passion and an appreciation for all.

Pema Chodron, "the ego seeks to divide and separate, spirit seeks to unify and heal."

Life becomes simpler as you surrender to the gentle winds of the universe and release the tentacles of society and all its conforming innuendos.

Mike Maples Jr., "ego is about who's right. Truth is about what's right."

A slow detachment from the material world will begin. You may experience 'lightness' and a lower volume from the ego. The ego will never quit trying to coerce you back 'into the fold'.

There is a 'magical' space during my meditation. An opening is made for stillness. I call this my egoless, my mask-less time. I try to bring this egoless feeling back into my reality with me when slowly transitioning from my silent space.

More the knowledge, lesser the ego
Lesser the knowledge, more the ego.

ALBERT EINSTEIN

. . .

WITH THE UNDERSTANDING OF THE EGO COMES endless possibilities. Recognizing when your ego is talking makes you selective of your words and actions. You identify toxic thinking patterns and shun them. The ego craves quantity, the soul desires only quality of life.

GANDHI, "YOU MUST BE THE CHANGE YOU WISH TO see in the world."

Thoughts/Memories

Deepak Chopra, "I use memories, but don't allow memories to use me."

There are numerous times in your life when you wish you had: smiled more, said kinder words, hugged, been positive, listened better, struggled less with emotions.

Understand, 'it is what it is'. Grow from these moments, allow these reflective times to propel you forward.

These moments are 'post-it' notes on your script. A deviation, a blimp, but back on your script you will go.

Focus on Maya Angelou's words of being "a rainbow in someone else's cloud."

Feel like a human radar, seeking out positive signs.

Your thoughts affect the significance of your life. I have made the conscious choice that it is not about the quantity of life but the quality of life. My 'light' seeks positivity and fulfilling my dharma.

Albert Einstein, "there are two ways to live your life, one as though nothing is a miracle. The other as though everything is a miracle."

My pure, positive thoughts come through meditation and 'my time' in nature. I am comforted when I feel the slow, gradual internal shift during 'my time'. These pauses are valuable to me. I am content within myself and do not have a need for external 'things'.

Tony Dungy, "be positive. Your mind is more powerful than you think. What is down in the well comes up in the bucket. Fill yourself with positive things."

Kind conversations are positive words chosen with care. Words that will travel to wherever encouraging words are needed.

Mark Twain, "kindness is the language the blind can see, and the deaf can hear."

Teaching was my prized vocation. I loved the chats, in the classroom, the exchange of words and thoughts. I find children are naturally positive and see rainbows all around them. They are optimistic, live mostly with peace and harmony within their body, mind, and soul.

I like to think our classroom was our sanctuary. When situations arose, we handled them in the classroom with affirmative reasoning. Our goal being: we all learn from each child's positive and negative words and actions.

Kristen Butler, "be thankful for every new challenge. Each will give you more strength, wisdom, and character."

Words and feelings of gratitude were my central theme as an educator, mother, and global citizen. Thank you and moments of 'awe' were the premise of my day in and outside of the classroom.

Shiv Khera, "your positive action combined with positive thinking results in success."

Thank you will 'light up' any situation.

John Wooden, "things turn out best for the people who make the best of the way things turn out."

"Laugh more and be more," is my personal mantra.

I love to laugh. I recognized that at an early age, humor could transition a negative scene into a positive one. Humor helps to dissipate negative thoughts and actions and replaces them with lightness. Humor allows you to see the world differently, with sparkling clear lights.

Napoleon Hill, "a positive mind finds a way it can be done. A negative mind looks for all the ways it can't be done."

I seek positive people, positive masks, and scene changes now. I am happiest with humor, healthy thoughts and actions that bring happiness to others. I encourage only positive self-talk. When negative words attempt to enter my internal space, I put wings on them.

I have had negative times on my life journey; I have concluded that I did not like that ME. I worked hard when I went off script to get back on script. My script and purpose are my lighthouse and are guiding me home now.

Mahatma Gandhi, "keep your values positive because your values become your destiny."

I know that with every mask and scene transition comes change. I have, with time, tried to embrace every change that my director, my higher self, my soul guided me through.

This guidance was administered with love and knowledge of my own personal life script. I learned to trust my intuition, my inner compass and inner light. They have served me well.

Marcus Aurelius, "the happiness in your life depends upon the quality of your thoughts."

Socrates, "the secret of change is to focus all of your energy not on fighting the old, but on building the new."

I believe the Universal Script will keep moving forward with new scenes and new mask transitions for all.

I hope you will embrace each scene and mask change with positive thoughts and actions, and when you do go off script, you will be guided back with 'love and light'.

JON KABAT-ZINN, "YOU CANNOT STOP THE WAVES, but you can learn to surf."

Loneliness

HAFIZ, "I WISH I COULD SHOW YOU WHEN YOU ARE lonely or in darkness the astonishing light of your own being."

Most people experience feelings of loneliness throughout their lives.

Some seek to be alone and wear their loneliness mask with ease.

For others, those feelings of needing to be separate or alone chiefly transpire during the transition of a mask and scene.

> *If you are feeling lonely, you know that you*
> *have:*
> *Books to nurture your mind*
> *Hands to create and explore*
> *Wind to calm your mind*
> *Breaths to soothe your nerves*
> *Nature to soak your worries away*
> *Stars to decorate your dreams.*
>
> EMMA XU

If you have left the flock and have sought other pastures to browse, by many you would be considered 'different' or, in Malcolm Gladwell's words, an "outlier."

Aldous Huxley, "if one's different, one's bound to be lonely."

The loner connects with their intuition more readily. They tend to find peace, companionship, and harmony within themselves.

Ralph Waldo Emerson, "nothing can bring you peace but yourself."

Sometimes you just need 'quiet time' or 'me time'. During these times, you take your inner staircase to find the room that is right for you.

Rumi, "don't feel lonely. The entire universe is inside you."

In this inner space, you reconnect with your higher self, your director.

You review your script, your next scene and mask change. Your director coaches and guides you for a potentially successful transition. You self-evaluate your life journey and tweak where you feel necessary.

You observe the story of your life thus far and recognize the lessons being taught to you by life.

Paulo Coelho, "if you are never alone, you cannot know yourself."

Loneliness can be a mask worn on the outside. Inside, however, you may enter a room where a dress rehearsal for your next scene is practiced and reviewed.

Mandy Hale, "a season of loneliness and isolation is when the caterpillar gets its wings."

The curtain will slowly rise—the new you transitions into your new space. The lonely mask fades as your new mask slowly evolves.

Janet Fitch, "loneliness allows your soul to grow."

The thought that the sun is alone but still shines brings comfort.

Perhaps introverts can wear this mask with greater ease than an extroverted personality.

Being alone is a powerful mask and is a master teacher for 'what life is', the connection to oneself.

Maxwell Maltz, "if you make friends with yourself, you will never be lonely."

As you move towards the last scenes of your life, you often crave loneliness. You have had many mask and scene changes. You have slowly been following your script and have transformed from a 'somebody' to a 'nobody' on your journey.

Your ego has retired; your soul has taken up residence.

Deepak Chopra, "if love is universal, no one can be left out."

You are evolving to ONE.

EINSTEIN, "ONE FEELS THE INSIGNIFICANCE OF THE individual and it makes me happy."

THE CURTAIN
LOWERS

Your Final Scenes

DEEPAK CHOPRA, "WE ARE DIVINE BEINGS. OUR soul's journey is to unite us into our human family. There is warmth in the collective consciousness and a feeling of being home. When in this realm, there is a feeling that all is perfect, all is well. Here we aspire for perfect health for all, experience joy and vitality. I am absolute existence. I am a field of all possibilities."

Your script and life journey have served you well. There comes a juncture where you acknowledge there is less time in front of you. You have a longing to be harmonious with your life and footprint.

You can sense the dimming of the lights and the last few curtain calls. There are subtle signs from your body and your environment.

You have found strength and inner harmony while challenging 'society's, chartered course'.

. . .

Helen Keller, "life is either a daring adventure or nothing. To keep our faces toward change and behave like free spirits in the presence of fate is strength and undefeatable."

Spiritual Journey

BHAGAVAD GITA, "HE WHO EXPERIENCES THE UNITY of life sees his own self in all beings, and all beings in his self."

Spiritualism is a journey.

A spiritual self has a feeling of vastness and immersion in their spiritual growth with little regard for physical 'things'.

Spiritual beings have wholesome personalities. They are not engaged in the material world. They are balanced individuals who love freely, are visionary, and display empathy toward all living entities.

Walter Isaacson wrote of Leonardo da Vinci, "despite his immersion into science, or perhaps because of it, Leonardo had developed an ever-deepening appreciation for the profound spiritual mystery of our place in the cosmos."

Individual spiritual sensory experiences are beyond human manifestations.

Your heart opens when wearing your spiritual mask. You witness unfairness and, in your own way, attempt to make life a 'bit better,' for the less fortunate.

Actions can involve visible gestures or invisible prayers and blessings.

You become a seeker and seek to become part of the whole. Nature is often your connector to this 'oneness' that you seek.

Albert Einstein, "look deep into nature, and then you will understand everything better."

You acknowledge the divinity within you. You love yourself. You love your temple.

Aberjhani, "dare to love yourself as if you were a rainbow with gold at both ends."

Your spiritual mask seeks peace, purpose and is at one with your script. All living things become your priority.

As my children would say, you only turn to the material world for 'supplies'.

Spiritual souls innately know we are all one and endeavor throughout their journey to honor this oneness.

Dr. Margaret Paul, let "kindness to all things be your light."

An understanding of infinity slowly evolves with the spiritual mask.

Ralph Waldo Emerson, "let the measure of time be spiritual, not mechanical."

A spiritual journey can be lonely. You feel different and avoid situations that accentuate your difference. There are times when you feel like an alien and wonder why you just cannot fit in.

James E Faust, "a rebirth out of spirituality adversity causes us to become new creatures."

You have coping masks you can wear in various uncomfortable social situations.

A spiritual journey is often isolating. It is suited to individuals rather than societies.

Martin Luther King Jr., "take the first step in faith. You don't have to see the whole staircase, just the first step."

Each step may involve a mask and scene change.

To be spiritual is to be a seeker. The light of science has opened infinite possibilities for a seeker. Seekers ask internal questions and move around the planet to find the answers.

Seekers pursue a path of unmasking their 'inner knowledge'.

Harari, "the quest usually begins with a question, who am I? The quest takes you in mysterious ways towards unknown destinations."

Seekers, seek truths and facts. They trust their intuition to guide them to where they need to go, to find the answers to their questions.

Seekers are 'open sages' and experience and play with new thoughts.

The spiritual journey beckons you throughout your life. It is written into your eternal script. If not accomplished in this life, perhaps the next?

Harari sees each journey as an "infinitesimally brief stay on our tiny speck of a planet."

There comes, through time, an alliance with your script.

Pema Chodron, "nothing ever goes away until it has taught us what we need to know."

With this understanding comes a resilience, a tenacious mask to learn the lesson presented.

Some ask: is this a human journey or a spiritual journey?

> *You have to grow from the inside out.*
> *None can teach you,*
> *None can make you spiritual.*
> *There is no other teacher,*
> *But your own soul.*

> SWAMI VIVEKANANDA

MY SPIRITUAL JOURNEY HAS TAKEN ME TO PLACES most people have not heard of. To remote villages and areas, many of which I cannot pronounce. Nevertheless, it is in these isolated places that I feel the most content and connected.

David Brooks, "spiritual seekers are not so easily satisfied and are determined to follow the big question wherever it leads – not to places you know well or wish to visit."

When I was in Nepal, working alongside village women to bring water to their community, we would chat through an interpreter.

Here, my spiritual journey deepened when a village woman imparted, "I like the words you speak."

In Nepal, one out of four children die from a water-borne disease.

In south India, around the community well, and north India, around the village pond, I experienced the 'oneness' of these communities. A lower self that was connected to universal wisdom.

It is here, in these remote villages, which few know of, and few would visit, my spiritual mask transitioned on.

Bernie Siegal sees spirituality as the "ability to find love, peace, and happiness in an imperfect world."

When trekking in Nepal, I heard of the trafficking of Sherpa children. Sherpas are known for their mountain climbing skills and ability to survive in high altitudes in the Himalayan Mountains. They are best known as guides and porters for wealthy climbers and tour operators.

The Sherpas set up the camps on Mount Everest; some lose their lives during the climb. They receive minimal wages for their hazardous labor. Few can support their families; few have any education. They do what they can to survive in an 'imperfect world'.

Perhaps spiritualism is a 'sticky note' on each life script. Many choose to remove and transfer it to a subsequent script in a later life experience.

It is an infinite life script on an infinite life journey.

Harari, "a journey in which we doubt the conventions and deals of the mundane world and walk towards an unknown destination."

We trust our inner compass to guide us each day to the answers to our questions on our way home.

Spiritual seekers pursue other paths, to escape the worldly order.

Spiritual travelers seek a journey that challenges outdated beliefs and conventions that do not satisfy their hunger for harmony for ALL.

At the center of your being
You have the answer
You know who you are
And you know
What you want.

RUMI

A SPIRITUAL JOURNEY IS AN INWARD QUEST. WORDS cannot describe this passage, so silence becomes your mask-less stance.

Deepak Chopra, "a spiritual seeker has no need for outer recognition. Inner fulfillment is enough."

This mask-less state is achieved when body, mind, and soul are in harmony with the universal script, which is choreographed by the heavenly music created by the stars and all that is.

As we approach the last scenes of this life experience, you recognize and cherish all the masks you have worn, all the scene changes, and how they were each necessary for your evolution.

You recognize the painful scenes and bless them for the lessons that life knew you required.

Rumi, "these pains you feel are messengers. Listen to them."

Your journey 'in' has begun and all the answers you seek for this lifetime are there.

Bernie Siegal, "with age, the external meaning vanishes."

You applaud yourself for facing many of your fears you met along the way on your journey and recognize in a Buddha teaching,

"Fear does not prevent death. It prevents life."

You know when you are in the right environment; the markers for your journey's success are there for those who seek them.

Ram Dass, "the next message you need is always right where you are."

Every day in a spiritual journey is new and exciting. Each day is a rebirth.

Our youngest son always greeted his new day with the words, "yippee! It is morning."

His words at such a young age captured my attention. I tried to walk his words.

Stanley Kunitz, "I can hardly wait for tomorrow. It means a new day for me each and every day."

Life leaves messages for us throughout our day. Learn to scan for them.

Bernie Singer envisions purple as a spiritual color. Perhaps it is saying, "I am ready for the spiritual transition."

Interestingly, my mother recounted that my older sister, who passed young, that her favorite color was purple.

A spiritual seeker is open to past and future lives.

Susan Orlean, "if you can see your life reflected in previous lives, and can imagine it reflected in subsequent ones, you can begin to discover order and harmony. You know that you are part of a larger story that has shape and purpose – a tangible, familiar past and a constantly refreshed future."

Finale

WE ARE ALL VISITORS TO THIS TIME, THIS PLACE.

> *We are just passing through*
> *Our purpose is to observe,*
> *To learn,*
> *To grow,*
> *To love,*
> *And then we return home.*

AUSTRALIAN ABORIGINAL PROVERB

THE STORY OF LIFE IS GROWING UP AND GROWING old.

There are signs that emerge, preparing you for the final scenes.

Cicero, "life is like a play. A good actor knows when to leave the stage."

For some it is retirement from a profession that you have loved. It was who you were.

I experienced this when retiring after a 32-year teaching career. A huge void surfaced that first September, as I watched the children returning to school. However, many masks and new scenes became available to me.

With retirement came a continuation of quality time, and I initiated this book. It began as a memoir for my children. The ideas flowed and, many scraps of paper with meaningful quotes that I cherished, were revisited.

An outline for All the World Is A Stage began, to appear through travel, helping, walks, bike rides, yoga, meditations, random chats and still times.

I read often, and in each book, there was a sign, a pearl for me. There were gems all around me, each day new 'magical' inspirations materialized.

I evolved to being Elizabeth Hay's, "lost wave seeking a forgotten shore."

I revisited the Akashic Records. It awakened something deep within me. I perceived it as an account of each of our lifetimes. Each narrative highlighted each soul's value to the ongoing universal script. An 'AWE' moment.

An additional idea that resonated with me, "birth is not a beginning, death is not an end" from Chuang Tzu.

Amor Towles, "life will find her in time, for eventually it finds us all."

Life found me, after I recognized and attained peace with my ego and society's controls.

My oldest son, as a teenager, said that he liked living in a 'multidimensional' world. I was taken back by his words, what did he mean?

I slowly began to understand his words, through my own journey.

Living in a one-dimensional world is safe, you know what the next day will generally be, your routines are set, few surprises.

Entering the multidimensional world, moves you from calm to rougher seas. There are numerous mask and scene changes, as life becomes unpredictable and fast moving. You learn to adjust your sails and to move into unchartered waters with ease and confidence.

Your world opens for you, as you surrender to your script.

Mark Twain, "I have lived a long life and had many troubles, most of which never happened."

My nomadic spirit slowly surfaced.

Elizabeth Hay, "no one belonged to a place, unless they were aboriginal. The rest of us are like dust of the earth blown east, west, north, south."

I was slowly releasing all my self-imposed constraints and societies expectations.

I favor the 'multidimensional' mask I am now wearing.

With openness, my faith and trust in my script was acknowledged.

Life became an adventure, each day a 'magical flying carpet'.

The Universal Script connects each one of us. Our script guides us in our growth, our transitions and helps us to evolve through our many shifts, over many reincarnations.

As we internally expand our awareness, our external reality transforms.

Rumi, "there is a voice that does not use words. Listen."

I listened and a whole new realm unfolded.

Susan Orlean, "in Senegal, the polite expression for saying someone died is to say his or her library has burned."

Or has their library not burned, but simply receded into the infinite Universal Script?

A Final Thought

BERNIE SIEGAL, "WHEN YOU WERE BORN, YOU CRIED, and the whole world rejoiced. Live your life in such a manner that when you die, the world cries and you rejoice."

A few years ago, I visited Brussels with my husband who was attending a conference.

At our last dinner, I met an interesting man who lived in New Delhi, India. We chatted about India. I told him about an upcoming 'helping' in Kolkata. He responded that his family home was in Kolkata.

Another 'awe' moment, a serendipitous moment. We exchanged email addresses.

As I approached the time to leave for Kolkata, I emailed our friend and we agreed to meet.

During many of the Kolkata sites, I was introduced to Swami Vivekananda's teachings. He was an Indian, Hindu monk. At one site we each had been given a small bust of his head, at another a colorful, framed picture, a book on Swami, then several more books.

When my friend picked me up, baggage and all, he noticed a Swami book in my bag.

I explained to him all the Swami 'things' I had acquired during my visit to Kolkata. He asked if I would like to visit Swami's home and temple. It was music to my ears, another adventure with the Swami.

We drove through the busy streets of Kolkata toward Swami's home and temple. We parked and walked into this pristine area. So unlike India! Flowers, cleanliness, few people, this was surreal to me.

We removed our shoes and walked into his temple.

It was beside the Ganga River. The temple was quiet and scarce of people. I walked slowly around and found a place where I could feel this soothing vibration. It was a feeling of home and peace. We lingered there.

My friend shared information about Swami Vivekananda. He was 39 and one day said to his disciples, "I am going to leave now."

He went to his chambers and did not return. When they found him several hours later, he had passed.

I learned through conversations and research about the word 'mahasamadhi', a Hindu and Yogic tradition. It is an act of consciously and intentionally leaving one's body.

Swami's cremated ashes were under the floor of the temple where we had been standing. My readings on Swami's passing concluded that Swami left through his meditation.

Harari, "if you want to understand death, you need to understand life."

It is reported that Albert Einstein refused surgery, "I have done my share; it is time to go."

My own father gave my mother a card, thanking her for his great life. He died suddenly thereafter.

Death is an inevitable universal process that eventually occurs in all organisms.

My biology teacher's words, "energy can neither be created nor destroyed" have echoed within me all my life.

Those words, that thought, were the essence of my life journey. They resonated within me at 18 and still do now in my 70s.

I believe death is your energy moving to the next room in the universe. Your life experiences 'noted' in the Universal Script.

Your thunderous Academy Award applause welcoming you home. Many congratulations for being the best actor or actress on the world stage.

Paulo Coelho, "we never lose our loved ones. They accompany us. They do not disappear from our lives. We are merely in different rooms."

No one eludes their final curtain call.

"Death is democratic", wrote Jose Guadalupe Posada, "at the end, regardless of whether you are white, dark, rich or poor, we all end up as skeleton."

The curtain lowers, we acknowledge our applause, we walk off the stage that has served us well.

You review your script, acknowledge good passages and scenes that need repair.

You eagerly await the next script that will be offered to you for your new entrance onto the world stage.

> *Perhaps they are not stars*
> *But rather openings in heaven*
> *Where the love of our loved ones*
> *Pour through and shine down upon us*
> *To let us know they are happy.*

INUIT PROVERB

VINCENT VAN GOGH WROTE TO HIS BROTHER THEO, "just as we take the train to go to Tarascon or Rouen, we take death to go to a star."

Thank You

I would like to thank you for your time and openness in reading All The World Is A Stage.

I hope there was a word, phrase, quote, or thought you permitted to be embedded deep within you.

Thank you to all the authors whose books and thoughts kindled my 'awakening'. You helped to release the gifts that came with me from the universe:

David Brook, Deepak Chopra, Angela Duckworth, Tom Friedman, Yuval Noah Harari, Elizabeth Hay, Walter Isaacson, Martin Luther King Jt., Stephen Pinker, Joseph Murphy, Susan Orlean, Bernie Siegel, Jen Sincero, Michael Singer, Eckhart Tolle, Arnold Weinstein

Thank you to all the souls for their quotes and poems, some collected and treasured from the age of 16:

Aberjhani, Sunday Adelaja, Joseph Addison, Aesop, Lailah Gifty Akita, Omar M Al-Aqeel, Danti Alighieri, Mata Amritanandamayi, Hans Christian Anderson, Maya Angelou, Guillaume Apollinaire, Louis Armstrong, St. Augustine, Marcus Aurelius, Johann Sebastian Bach, James Baldwin, Henry Ward Beecher, Susan J Bissonette, William Blake, Robert Bresson, Brene Brown, Dan Brown, Pierce Brown, Elizabeth Barrett Browning, Robert Browning, Bill Bryson, Buddha, Sabine

Buhlmann, Richard Burton, Kristen Butler, Octavia E Butler, Thomas Carlyle, Willa Carter, Pablo Casals, Pierre Teilhard de Chardin, Mary Ellen Chase, Ruben Chavez, Pema Chodron, Dick Clark, Leonard Cohen, Christopher Columbus, Confucius, Paulo Coelho, Mason Cooley, E.E. Cummings, Ram Dass, Wade Davis, Robert Delaunay, Panache Desai, Charles Dickens, Emily Dickerson, Walt Disney, Mike Dooley, Frederick Douglass, Tom Dungy, Meister Eckhart, Albert Einstein, Queen Elizabeth, T. S. Elliott, Ralph Waldo Emerson, Epicurus, James E Faust, Janet Fitch, Ann Frank, Benjamin Franklin, Robert Frost, Margaret Fuller, Mahatma Gandhi, Paul Gauguin, Francesca Gino, Bhagavad Gita, Malcolm Gladwell, Johann Wolfgang von Goethe, Vincent Van Gogh, Jennifer Gray, Kyle Gray, Edgar Guest, Hafiz, Mandy Hale, Thich Nhat Hanh, Nathaniel Hawthorne, Georg Wilhelm Friedrich Hegel, Heinrich Heine, Heraclitus, Rabbi Heschel, Napolean Hill, Hippocrates, Sam Horn, Aldous Huxley, Muhammad Iqbal, William James, Criss Jami, Carl Jung, Immanuel Kant, John Keating, Helen Keller, Munia Khan, Shiv Khera, Mastin Kipp, Stanley Kunitz, Aung San Suu Kyi, Dalai Lama, Anne Lamott, Frederick Lenz, Abraham Lincoln, Christopher Logue, James Russell Lowell, Krish K Madembeth, Ramana Maharshi, Maxwell Maltz, Nelson Mandela, Mike Maples Jr., Bill McNabb, Jillian Michaels, John Milton, Michel de Montaigne, Maria Montessori, Wolfgang Amadeus Mozart, Debasish Mridha, John Muir, Mark Nepo, Isaac Newton, John Newton, Friedrich Nietzsche, Anais Nin, Novalis, Barack Obama, Catherine O'Meara, Dr. Margaret Paul, St. Paul, Pablo Picasso, Plato, Jose Guadalupe Posada, Lawrence Clark Powell, Marcel Proust, Pythagoras, Sangeeta Rana, Fred Rogers, Eleanor Roosevelt, Theodore Roosevelt, Rumi, Peter Santos, Robert Schuller, Wilfrid Sellars, Dr. Seuss, William Shakespeare, George Bernard Shaw, Harrison Small, Oliver

Small, Socrates, Robert Lewis Stevenson, Radhanath Swami, Mother Teresa, Henry David Thoreau, Kevin J Todeschi, Leo Tolstoy, Dr. Stephane Treyvaud, Desmund Tutu, Mark Twain, Lao Tzu, Chuang Tzu, Brenda Ueland, Vangelis, Denis Waitley, , Simon Weil, Edith Wharton, Walt Whitman, Marianne Williamson, E.O. Wilson, John Wooden, Virginia Woolf, Wordsworth, Emma Xu, W. B. Yeats, Malala Yousafzai, Zen, Jon Kabat- Zinn

Thank you to each student who shared a classroom with me. Thank you for your patience with me and teaching me everything I know.

Thank you to all the souls who smile back.

Thank you to all my angels invisible and visible.

Thank you to all my friends from birth to infinity.

Thank you to all the places I visited and the vibrations you shared with me.

Thank you to nature and your 'knowing' magic.

Thank you to my bikes and our rides together.

Thank you to all my dogs, cat, birds, and all animals who each spoke to me with your uplifting and helping energies.

Thank you to my body for always healing well and carrying me on my journey.

And thank you to my family, who gave me the freedom to be me.

Thank you to everyone and everything I did not mention. Suexxoo

Bibliography

Akemi, G. Why We Are Born. CreateSpace, 2014

Allende, Isabel. The Long Petal of the Sea. Bloomsbury, 2019

Bregman, Rutger. Humankind. Bloomsbury, 2020.

Brown, Dee. Bury My Heart at Wounded Knee. New York: Holt, Rinehart and Winston, 1970.

Brook, David. The Second Mountain. Penguin Books Australia, 2019.

Bryson, Bill. The Body. Penguin Random House Canada, 2019.

Cameron, Julia. The Artist's Way. TarcherPerigee, 1992.

Carson, Clayborne. The Autobiography of Martin Luther King Jr. Grand Central, 1998.

Chopra, Deepak. & Kafatos, Menas. You Are the Universe. Harmony, 2017.

Cicero, Marcus Tullius. How to Grow Old (ancient wisdoms for the second half of life). Princeton University Press, 2016.

Correa, Armando Lucas. The German Girl. Simon and Schuster 2016.

Davis, Wade. Light at the Edge of the World. Douglas and McIntyre Ltd. 2007.

Davis, Wade. The Wayfinders. House of Anansi, 2009.

Dispenza, Joe. Becoming Supernatural. Hay House Inc., 2019.

Doeer, Anthony. All the Light We Can Not See. Scriber, 2014.

Duckworth, Angela. Grit. Simon and Schuster, 2016

Durkan, David. Penguins on Everest. Swami Kailash, 2016.

Eger, Edith. The Choice. Simon and Schuster, 2017.

Friedman, Thomas. Thank You for Being Late. Farrar, Straus and Giroux, 2016.

Gandhi, Mahatma. An Autobiography of Mahatma Gandhi. Navajivan Mudranalaya, 1927.

Gates, Melinda French. The Moment of Lift. Macmillan, 2019.

Gladwell, Malcolm. Outliers. Little, Brown and Company. 2008

Gratz, Alan. Refugee. Scholastic, 2017.

Haben, Girma. Haben. Hachette Book Group, 2019.

Harari, Yuval Noah. Homo Deus. Harvill Secker, 2016.

Harari, Yuval Noah. Sapiens. Harper, 2014

Harari, Yuval Noah. 21 Lessons for the 21 Century. Spiegel and Gau, 2018

Hawkins, David. Letting Go: The Pathway of Surrender. Hay House, 2014

Bibliography

Hay, Elizabeth. Late Nights on Air. McClelland and Stewart, 2007.

Isaacson, Walter. Einstein. Simon and Schuster, 2007.

Isaacson, Walter. Leonardo da Vinci. Simon and Schuster, 2017.

Kaku, Michio. The Future of the Mind. Doubleday, 2014.

Kotb, Hoda. I Really Needed This Today. G. P. Putnam's Sons, 2019.

Krznaric, Roman. The Good Ancestor. The Experiment, 2020.

Larson, Erik. The Splendid and the Vile. Crown, 2020.

McRaven, William H. Make Your Bed. Hachette, 2017.

Moyes, JoJo. The Giver of Stars. Marketplace, 2019.

Murphy, Joseph. The Cosmic Power Within You. Penguin Random House, 1968.

Myss, Caroline. Invisible Acts of Power. Atria Books, 2006

Orlean, Susan. The Library Book. Simon Schuster, 2019.

Patchett, Ann. The Dutch House. Harper, 2019.

Peterson, Jordan. Twelve Rules For life. Random House, 2018.

Pinker, Stephen. Enlightenment Now. Penguin Books, 2018

Siegel, Bernie S. Love, Medicine and Miracles. HarperCollins, 1986.

Siegel, Bernie S. A Book of Miracles. HarperCollins, 2011

Silva, Daniel. The Order. HarperCollins, 2020.

Sincero, Jen. You Are a Bad Ass. Simon Schuster, 2013.

Sincero, Jen. You Are a Bad Ass at Making Money. Simon Schuster, 2017.

Singer, Michael. The Untethered Soul. New Harbinger, 2007.

Tolle, Eckhart. The Power of Now. Namaste, 1997.

Tolle, Eckhart. A New Earth. Viking, 2005.

Tolan, Sandy. The Lemon Tree. Penguin Random House, 2008.

Towles, Armor. Gentleman in Moscow. Viking, 2016.

Weinstein, Arnold. Morning, Noon and Night. Random House, 2011.

Wilkerson, Isabel. Caste. Penguin Random House, 2020.

ARTICLES

Burton, Robert. The Anatomy of Melancholy. BBC, 1628 text

Crossley-Baxter, Lily. The Untranslatable Word That Connects Wales. BBC Travel, Feb. 12, 2021

Gino, Francesca. The Business Case for Curiosity. Harvard Business. Review, Sept-Oct. 2018.

New York Times, We Have More Than Five Senses. March 15, 1964.

Printed in Great Britain
by Amazon

31662225R00133